Confessions and Reflections
of a Traveler

# Confessions and Reflections of a Traveler

*by*

BRETT R. MCLEAN

IONA

Iona Press
Vancouver, British Colombia

© 2010 by B.R. McLean

Published by Iona Press
Vancouver, BC, Canada
ionapress@gmail.com

Printed in Canada, United Kingdom, USA, and Australia.

All Rights Reserved. No part of this publication may be reproduced, stored in a retrieval system, or transmitted in any form or by any means—for example, electronic, photocopy, recording—without the prior written permissions of the publisher. The only exception is brief quotations in printed reviews.

Scripture quotations are from The Holy Bible, English Standard Version, copyright © 2001 by Crossway Bibles, a division of Good News Publishers. Used by permission. All rights reserved.

cover art: Jessica Bell www.jessicabellart.com

ISBN 978-0-9867127-0-8

*for him*

# *Contents*

Acknowledgements..................................................................ix

CHAPTER 1    *Beginnings*..........................................................13

CHAPTER 2    *Lost*..................................................................23

CHAPTER 3    *Middle Earth and Ontology (Ontology)*............37

CHAPTER 4    *The Bug goes South*..........................................75

CHAPTER 5    *To Press or not to Press (Epistemology)*............91

CHAPTER 6    *Pipes and Prophets*..........................................125

CHAPTER 7    *Trouble in Paradise (Ethics)*............................143

CHAPTER 8    *California Dreaming*........................................177

CHAPTER 9    *The End of Things (Teleology)*........................195

CHAPTER 10   *The Bug goes East*..........................................227

CHAPTER 11   *The Hope of Redemption*................................243

CHAPTER 12   *Mercer and Beyond*........................................273

Select Bibliography..............................................................297

Topical Index......................................................................303

# *Acknowledgments*

This book describes an epic journey but the writing of the book was equally an epic journey. A journey in learning and faith with the goal of doing what I thought was impossible. Thanks to all who helped and encouraged me to keep going forward.

Jason Bull for challenging me to write. Susan Kennedy-Carter for your tremendous work in the earlier stages of this manuscript and encouraging me as a writer. Without your efforts I would be a lesser writer and this would be a lesser book. Genvieve Gagne-Hawes for your work in the final stages of the manuscript edit. This is a much improved work as a result of your editing and critique.

Jeff Boldt for your influence on me in the areas of Theology and Philosophy and your critique of Chapters Three and Five. Apart from your influence this book may have taken eight years rather than four. The group who read through the manuscript at PGCC; Lori, Louise, Jerry, Gin, Cathy, Rachel and Jason for your critique; Greg Laing for your encouragement and logistical support. Jessica Bell for your inspired work on the cover. The final product exceeded my expectations and then some.

Books don't get written in vacuums and although I spent many hours alone typing, the following communities and individuals were important relational supports through the writing and editing process.

Vancouver: Phil and Elona Weil, Mike Root, Alec Arnold, Teresa Davis, Jenny Koh, Ginimi Chan, Tom Rudzinski, Gregor Cantz, Jason Bull, and Jeff Boldt. The Maple Group; Andrew & Corinna Nairn, Cathy Bowering, Peter Matsubara, Rachael Sawatzky, Jim Mier, Amy and Stef Klassen, and Kenneth Chan.

Toronto: Jacob & Anna Buurma. Kingston: The Lyon family and friends.

London: Ikoh, Ben, Dan, Tim & Tiffany, and the Skrentny family. The Holloway Group: Ros, Ikoh, Frank, Tomi, Mary, Tim & Tiffany, Jen, Sherrie, Hannah, and Sarah.

Rome and Milan: The Weil family and Kenneth Chan.

Perth: my mother Carol McLean for your support and hospitality, John McLean, Barry McLean, Lyn and Neville.

Singapore: Hannah, Sarah, Claude, and Priscilla.

The many and various coffee shops that I wrote most of this book in: The Blue Parrot on Granville Island, Blenz on Bayswater and Broadway, Starbucks in Mayfair and Tottenham, and The Merchant in Rockingham.

BRETT R. MCLEAN

The trip narrated in this book is based on true events and the names of all significant characters (apart from myself) and some minor ones have been changed.

# CHAPTER 1

## *Beginnings*

Raindrops steadily dotted the windscreen as The Bus made its way through the rolling hills of Pennsylvania. A grey mist loomed above the valley, but after weeks of planning and looking forward to this trip, nothing could dampen our spirits. Our summer adventure had officially begun.

It was the summer of '96, and Nate and I were on our way to Atlanta, Georgia. The vehicle that was to take us on this trip was

Nate's '69 Volkswagen Bus. The Bus was white and in relatively good condition—except it burnt a lot of oil; we needed to add some every 200 miles or so. On the front window was a sticker of a purple bear, the icon of the band *The Grateful Dead.* Over the years Nate had built a fond relationship with The Bus, and he spoke of it like an old friend with a life and being of its own.

The great thing about The Bus was that I could be sitting in the passenger seat, get up, walk to the back, and go to sleep, all whilst The Bus was in motion. I could also do this in reverse, and sometimes I would wake up to the familiar hum of the engine as Nate drove us to the next destination. I loved the experience of traveling without even getting out of bed.

The Volkswagen Bus was something of a chick magnet back in the day, but by 1996 its magnetism had been lost. The hippie era in which The Bus had been such an icon had passed, and The Bus was now a relic of a bygone time. In the 70's the occupants of a bus has been considered hip and cool, but twenty years later, we were perceived as poor prospects for modern North American women: financially unstable, low career potential, and, more than likely, drug addicts.

I had no idea then that the trip ahead would have such an impact on my life. Since the summer of '96, I have taken many trips and had many adventures, but now they all seem to stand in the shadow of this one. Prior to this trip I was in a state of confusion about who I was, uneasy about the future I'd planned for myself.

The coincidental nature of how the trip came to be has always astonished me. Halfway through the spring semester at Penn

State in 1996, I had planned to spend my summer furthering my career as a mechanical engineer with an internship at a pipe factory in Pennsylvania. The internship fell through, however, and the summer suddenly open before me.

Nate lived on the same floor as me in Beaver Hall (a dormitory at Penn State), but we hadn't interacted much during the term. During the winter semester my life was busy, and I never found a daily rhythm; I fit in even showers whenever I could—usually at odd hours. For some bizarre reason, Nate was on the same random shower schedule I was; one night we were both showering at 8:23 PM, and a few nights later we were there at 1:05 AM. After about two months of meeting like this, we began our friendship.

But on the second-to-last day of term, Nate and I were still more acquaintances than friends. Hanging out in the recreation room on our floor, we got to talking about our summer plans.

"So what are you up to this summer, Nate?"

"Well, I need to paint my dad's house in Mercer, but after that things are pretty open. What are you up to?"

"I was planning to do an internship but that kind of fell through. I'm not really sure at this stage— I thought it might be good to do some traveling around the USA."

"Hey man, I was thinking same thing after I finished the painting job. Are you up for helping me paint my house and then traveling together?"

"Ahh...sure—you got a car?"

"Even better man, I've got a Volkswagen Bus—the perfect adventuring vehicle for a trip around the States!"

"Well, all right then, let's do it!" I said.

In the course of a ten-minute conversation, Nate and I had agreed to spend the whole summer together. If our relationship was somewhat uncertain then, by the end of that summer it would be certain—for better or worse. After exams were over I packed up my room and gathered my belongings for the summer ahead. Nate drove The Bus to Beaver Hall and before long we were on our way to Mercer.

Mercer was one of those quiet countryside towns where you wished you could spend the rest of your life. After a few hours in The Bus with Nate, I went from living with more than 40,000 other students to a town of just over 2,000 people. In Mercer nobody was in a hurry. The mild yet bright summer days and the communal attitude made it a small paradise for me.

Our daily schedule in Mercer was to get up, have breakfast, and work on painting the house. Nate's Dad, Rick, had commissioned the painting job and always made sure we had sufficient blue paint and brushes. Rick's schedule involved a lot of time at work and a lot of time on the couch sleeping or watching television. I didn't have much interaction with him, but I felt the house painting was important to him and he was inwardly happy that I was working on it.

Nate was the youngest member of the family; he had an older sister who also lived at the house. In staying with Nate's family, I sensed they harbored some issues. Nate's mom died when he was young, leaving a void in the family that had yet to be filled. Nate had a somewhat distant relationship with his father, which struck me as unusual because they had done trips in The Bus together. Despite these underlying issues, however, I was welcomed into the family and enjoyed staying there.

Nate and I spent the first month of the summer scraping off old paint and sloshing on the new. The house was large, and putting on three coats of paint kept us busy. We did, however, have time for fun—and with Nate, there were always a multitude of options. On the odd occasion when nothing much was doing, somebody would stop by, a random stranger even, and we would suddenly have a new friend. In Mercer there was always an adventure to be had or a person to visit.

Unlike the bustling Penn State campus, everyone knew everyone in Mercer. One person that Nate wished he knew a little better was the local preacher's daughter up the road. Nate had a longstanding interest in her, but her dad was a roadblock. He didn't see Nate as the ideal mate—and possibly neither did she. I got the sense that a lot of girls humored Nate and enjoyed his company but didn't share his romantic intentions.

On some nights, we stayed with Nate's quirky Uncle Synick. Uncle Synick was something of a second father to Nate, and the two of them got on really well. The Bus would roll up the driveway at Uncle Synick's, Nate's eyes alive with anticipation. I don't remember much about the layout of his uncle's house, but one of the first things that struck me was an indoor drying rack filled with rather large underwear.

"Hi Uncle Synick," Nate would yell.

"Hey Nate," Uncle Synick would shout from a far-off recess of his enormous house. Whatever was going on in Uncle Synick's life at that instant would stop, and moments later we would all be sitting at the table talking about the events of the day.

Once seated, we always spoke about our upcoming summer adventure. Uncle Synick would sit, taking in our excitement and energy.

"So how is the painting going?"

"Well, we're on the second coat right now; I think at this rate we're going to be on the road to Atlanta in a few weeks," Nate said, and away the conversation went.

Uncle Synick seemed to lead an ordinary-enough life but Nate was fascinated with all the goings-on nonetheless. I liked Uncle Synick; he was interesting and somewhat comical at the same time. He lived alone in a large house filled with broken-down appliances in need of repair and antiques accumulating dust. Uncle Synick seemed to be having the time of his life in his old age. After a night at his place we would wake up, have breakfast, jump into The Bus, and resume painting the house.

Painting was therapeutic for me. I loved being outside. Renewing a wall with color was somehow rejuvenating. As the sun slowly traversed a path across the sky and the birds chirped in the nearby trees, each stroke of the paintbrush renewed me. As much as I enjoyed the world of mechanical engineering, hours and hours of problems, equations, and variables took a toll on me. Engineering's focus on the ordered and predictable had stripped some of the wonder and mystery from my life.

In the world of engineering, my life was about solving problems, *doing* and *achieving*, but when my sole task was to paint the walls of a house, I felt I was able to get off the treadmill of achieving goals and begin *being*. At the time I had no idea who Martin Heidegger was (or for that matter, who any of the other philosophers that will come up in this book were), but I was experiencing something of the *being there* Heidegger writes about in *Being and Time*.

It had been a challenging semester for me at Penn State. Engineering had taken its toll, but I was also fitting into a new culture and place: I had arrived from Australia in January to complete my third year of mechanical engineering. I liked the change of scenery, but it was challenging to place myself relationally among so many other students in such a short period of time.

And even beyond this immediate change, something deeper was troubling me. As I thought about my life and existence, my future plans, something felt majorly wrong, but I had no idea what. I had thought certain things and goals would fill the void, but it remained no matter what I did. In coming to Penn State I believed I would get a different perspective on life and perhaps resolve the dissatisfaction eating me up from the inside.

In many ways I felt like John Locke in *Lost*[1], who you will meet in Chapter Two. Locke; disabled and working at a box factory, was also dissatisfied with his existence. He decided that he needed to go on an Australian walkabout in order for things to change. Like Locke on his venture, I had no idea how spending an exchange year in the States would solve my issues, but I believed that I needed to go. By the end of my first semester I couldn't say that I had found any answers, although my interest in spiritual writings began to grow at the end of term.

Life in Mercer was thus a great change for me. I felt like I had joined Nate's family and inherited Nate's friends, at least for the time I was there. By spending my days out painting and being

---

[1] *Lost*, creators: J.J. Abrams, Jeffrey Lieber, Damon Lindelof, ABC Studios, 2004, DVD.

with Nate, it was almost like I had entered a different existence. It was a great change from the tensions and pressures of a semester at Penn State. In fact, I enjoyed Mercer so much that I would not have minded spending the whole summer there. But after a month, Nate and I were both keen to get on the road and explore.

As The Bus slowly wound its way through the hills of Pennsylvania, I felt things were changing—somehow I was in the process of entering a different existence. The way I had seamlessly fit into living life at Mercer and the bizarre way Nate and I had decided to even do the trip suggested something beyond my comprehension at work. Despite the clouds looming, I eagerly anticipated the summer ahead.

# CHAPTER 2

# *Lost*

Dressed in a shirt and tie, Jack Shephard awakens suddenly. Above him tower leafy palm trees, swaying and rustling in the breeze, shielding him from the brilliant blue sky. Mangled tropical plants press against his back; the uncomfortable humidity makes him sweat in his torn suit, a relic from another world. As he begins to move, Jack feels like he has been hit by a train.

For a brief moment Jack wonders if he is dreaming. A vague memory of flying on an airplane flashes in his head. He remembers downing a whisky—then the terror of plummeting towards the earth on board Flight Oceanic 815. When Jack is no longer able to convince himself what he sees is a dream, he starts to wonder about the fate of the other passengers. Despite his whole body protesting, he slowly stands and begins running through the jungle.

Jack is no stranger to difficult situations. He is a gifted spinal surgeon who thrives under pressure. Under the tutelage of his father, Christian, Jack is one of the top spinal surgeons at St. Sebastian Hospital in Los Angeles. After a few minutes running through the jungle, Jack suddenly stops, brought to a halt by the sight of a never ending ocean. For a brief moment he is calmed by the vast body of water. Then the screams of distressed survivors reach his ears. Turning his head towards the commotion on the beach, the spectacular wreckage of Oceanic 815 overwhelms him. After determining who is in the most danger, Jack runs to help the survivors.

John Locke was also on Oceanic 815, a few rows behind Jack. While Jack was pitched into the jungle, Locke found himself lying on the beach surrounded by frantic fellow survivors and large pieces of the crashed plane. As Locke begins to move, he momentarily forgets the surrounding chaos, transfixed by his newfound ability to move his feet.

Four years ago Locke was pushed through an eight-story window. Confined to a wheel chair ever since, Locke went to Australia in hopes of going on a walkabout in the Outback. Locke felt convinced this was his destiny, and he did not inform the tour guide of his condition. His hopes were crushed, however, when the guide refused to take him due to his disability. The only thing Locke could do was return to the States.

On board Oceanic 815 Locke was a defeated man. He thought the walkabout would change things, but that hope had vanished. Given his circumstances, Locke would have been happy to die in the plane crash. But his fortunes were about to undergo a drastic change: he survived the plane crash and miraculously regained his ability to walk. Many of his fellow survivors are shell-shocked after the crash; Locke is delirious with happiness. As he rises and discovers the wonder of standing up, Jack spots him and asks for help assisting a wounded survivor.

Jack and Locke are both characters from the TV series *Lost*.[1] For the seventy-two survivors of Oceanic 815, the trauma of the plane crash is just the beginning of an eventful stay on The Island. As well as a lurking Island Monster and tropical polar bears, the Losties encounter strange visions, dreams, miracles, healings, and bizarre stories of other people who ended up on The Island. The Island seems to possess a mysterious life and being of its own.

A few days after the crash the Losties find the pilot, who tells them that six hours after the plane left Sydney he lost communication with air control. No one could track the plane on radar. In order to correct this problem, the pilot diverted the plane towards Fiji; at the time of the crash he estimates they were about one-thousand miles off course. Even the most diligent of rescues would not spread its net one-thousand miles.

Despite their slim hope of rescue, a group of Losties hike to

---

[1] *Lost*, creators: J.J. Abrams, Jeffrey Lieber, Damon Lindelof, ABC Studios, 2004, DVD.

a high point on The Island to see what they can pick up on the plane's transceiver. After an encounter with a ravenous polar bear, the hiking group reaches a high point. Turning on the transceiver, Sayid detects a signal, spoken in French, coming from The Island.

With Shannon interpreting, the group discovers that the signal is actually a distress call set to repeat, saying, "Please help me… Please come get me. I am alone now… I am on the island alone… Please someone come… The others are dead… It killed them… It killed them all." The message's iteration number is 17294531. It is on a thirty-second loop. Sayid calculates that the message has been playing for sixteen and a half years. After the group hears Shannon's translation, Charlie voices the fear they all feel: "Guys, where are we?"

Charlie's question becomes an ongoing question for the Losties who survive the perils of The Island. As the days turn into weeks and hopes of rescue fade, the Losties often wonder about The Island and how they are meant to interpret their existence there. Some of the Losties believe they are being punished; others believe destiny brought them to The Island. Still others believe they are there through pure chance.

Jack emerges as the primary leader of The Losties, but he finds it difficult to deal with the questions their bizarre circumstances raise. Jack is a man of reason. Jack interprets their crash landing as an unlucky break and believes that he and the other Losties are extremely lucky to have survived. Jack acknowledges that The Island is a little strange, but he believes there are logical explanations for everything. Jack's leadership of The Losties is centered on finding a way to get off The Island and resuming life in the real world.

Locke, who has been miraculously healed, believes the plane crash was meant to happen and that there is an underlying reason each of the Losties is on The Island. Locke is a man of faith. Locke undergoes a remarkable transformation as a result of the plane crash; the defeated man who boarded Oceanic 815 becomes a confident leader. Locke is not without his faults, but the Losties begin to see him as someone with an understanding of The Island.

As the weeks turn to months, some of the Losties become convinced that Jack's interpretation of The Island does not sufficiently explain their experience. There is something about The Island pure reason cannot encompass. While Jack assists the Losties with physical survival, he leaves them with a void in regard to understanding The Island's mysteries and the meaning of their existence there.

Ultimately, Jack's refusal to adequately deal with questions raised by strange happenings on The Island causes some of the Losties to reject him and embrace Locke as their leader. Even though Locke lacks many of Jack's leadership qualities, some of the Losties feel that Locke has a better understanding of The Island. The Losties don't just turn to Locke as a philosophical upgrade, however; they turn to Locke because they believe their very survival depends upon having a leader who understands the Island.

The dissatisfaction some of the Losties felt with Jack is similar to the dissatisfaction I experienced during the term at Penn State and, previously, in Australia. The answers I had been given in regard to my existence did not seem to line up with my experience of the world. When I thought about my existence and who I was, a big piece of the puzzle seemed to be missing.

Douglas Adams' *The Hitchhikers Guide to the Galaxy* book series is a humorous parody of the situation in which modern humans find themselves. The main character, Arthur Dent, manages to escape the Earth seconds before it is destroyed by the evil Vogons. Arthur is beamed up to one of the Vogon spaceships with the help of his friend Ford Prefect (who turns out to be an alien). Soon after his rescue Arthur learns that he is the only human being left in the universe.

Arthur is subsequently told that the Earth was actually a seven-million year project, designed by mice, to determine the ultimate question of life. Unfortunately the project was unintentionally foiled by the Vogons, who destroyed the earth seconds before the seven-million year cycle was complete. Arthur, the last human, survives. Within him is the ultimate question. The mice find out about Arthur's survival and pursue him.

Prior to their Earth project, the mice constructed the supercomputer Deep Thought in order to find out the meaning of life. After two million years of computation, Deep Thought told the mice the answer to the meaning of life was "42". Thoroughly disappointed with this answer, the mice were told by their creation that they needed to seek the ultimate question to which 42 provided the answer. Thus the Earth was created.

*The Hitchhikers Guide to the Galaxy* parodies the fruitless search for the meaning of life in which Arthur Dent is inextricably caught up. As the meaningless existence of planets and civilizations is recounted and the end of the universe is witnessed nightly from *The Restaurant at the End of the Universe* (the second book in the series), the reader is jarred by the random and unpredictable nature of existence according to Adams.

After reading several books by Adams, one is tempted to think that we can perhaps just go through life humoring ourselves at the idea of finding any ultimate meaning. Why bother with big questions when we can simply enjoy life and laugh a little along the way? In the modern era we have a decent understanding of the intricacies of our world and ourselves; why bother with big unanswerable questions? By simply leaving well-enough alone we avoid all manner of controversy and division.

It is true that ignoring questions about the meaning of life avoids social discomfort, but at the same time it creates internal angst and dissatisfaction akin to what I experienced before my trip with Nate. At the time I did not know what the big questions were. Still I felt the weight of them. The events of the summer of 1996 changed me. In reflecting on that summer, I see that the big questions concerning our existence do matter. Immediately after the summer, I shared my story with almost anyone who asked; over the years I have often wondered about other people experiencing similar tensions.

Everyone has to walk their own path, but along the way it is comforting to meet and talk with people who have taken similar journeys. Although I may not have met you in person, if you have read this far I am pretty sure you are on a somewhat similar path to the one I was on. Out of my desire to share some of the experiences from my trip with Nate and my reflections on my journey, I have written this book.

As I reflected on my life, I became aware that I made many assumptions about my existence without realizing. If the assumptions we make in life can be thought of as mountains, I was traveling though life without noticing the large mountain range through which I was walking. The going was fine on the plains, but when I started traversing the invisible mountains my journey became very difficult.

I came to realize that there are four large peaks in the philosophic mountain range which impact all of the other assumptions we make in life. These peaks represent assumptions or questions that have been discussed since philosophy began: *Ontology* (or the nature of reality); *Epistemology* (study of knowledge and how we can know things); *Ethics* (study of human action); and *Teleology* (the purpose or end of things). In a similar way to *The Hitchhikers Guide to the Galaxy*, we often have answers for these assumptions without really understanding the questions.

Understanding *Ontology*, *Epistemology*, *Ethics* and *Teleology* is by no means an easy task. To attempt to fully explain just one of them in a book this size would be considered a tall order. But these assumptions are so important to how we understand our existence that gaining a basic understanding of them is worthwhile. My aim in writing about these assumptions is to help the proverbial "man in the street" gain such understanding.

To explain these assumptions, I use the Losties and characters from *The Lord of the Rings* by J.R.R Tolkien as illustrations.[2] Although characters from these stories live in different, fantastic worlds, they also try to make sense of the reality in which they find themselves. We can benefit from their experiences and reflections.

---

[2] In using *Lost* and *Lord of the Rings* in my illustrations spoilers for those who do not already know these stories are unavoidable. Through reading this book, however, you will gain interesting insights into both stories and I hope enjoy them even more.

Familiarity with *Lost* or *The Lord of the Rings* is not essential for understanding this book, but knowing these stories will make my illustrations more vivid.

In addition to the Losties and characters from *The Lord of the Rings,* I will also interact with various philosophers. Philosophers can seem intimidating to the most educated of people, but in essence they are travelers like you and me, trying to understand the world in which they find themselves. They see and experience the same things we do and formulate various interpretations of that reality as a result.

Philosophers are curious characters. They dwell in caves and little cabins throughout the philosophical mountain range, but they are often seen on the four peaks in conversation with other philosophers. Although they live in little caves and cabins, their names are known in large cities and universities. Their ideas have a way of growing legs and migrating into large population centers. They seem to multiply and change as they travel, at times becoming unrecognizable from the idea that left the cabin or cave. The ideas of philosophers are important because each offers an interpretation of the different peaks representing the four big assumptions. Sometimes philosophers have slightly different takes on the terrain of the mountain; at other times you wonder if the philosophers are even talking about same mountain.

Over the course of reading this book you will begin to see that I like some philosophers more than others. Over the years I too have formed my views about each of the mountains, and I find that I get on better with those philosophers who think similarly. I don't apologize for this; it makes sense that a certain philosopher who helps me better navigate the philosophic mountains is one with whom I will stay longer to converse.

One of the philosophers I am going to talk about is Martin Heidegger (1889-1976), who posed the question, *"Why is there something rather than nothing?"* This is a great question to get us started. However we interpret our world and existence, we all have to deal with this question. It goes beyond *what* is there and asks *why* anything is there to begin with. Could there just as easily be nothing? Why do we exist when we could just as easily not exist? As we think about our world and existence it is important to ask the *what* question. However, we won't fully understand *what* is there until we ask *why* it is there.

Consider an illustration from the world of art: *La Gioconda,* better known as *The Mona Lisa,* by Leonardo Da Vinci, is perhaps the most famous painting ever produced. When we look at this painting we see a woman sitting in front of a background. To begin understanding this woman, we might examine the background for an idea of where she is and at what time she was alive. We may then look at the woman herself and ask: What is her age? What is she communicating to us by her facial expression? What is her pose? Does she appear confident or timid? What clothes is she wearing and what do those clothes say about her? It is also worth paying attention to the paint colors and brush strokes: are the color boundaries clearly defined or are they more fluid?

There are many more "what" questions we can ask, but we will not get far in understanding the painting until we ask the *why* question. Why has Da Vinci painted this particular woman? Was he paid to do so or did he just take an interest in her? Why did he paint her in this particular background? Why has he painted this particular expression on the face of the woman rather than a multitude of others? Why was this picture so important to Da Vinci?[3] Why has this painting so captured the public imagination?

Ultimately the *why* questions help us unlock the painting's meaning. The *what* questions help us formulate the *why* questions, but only the *why* questions enable us to really understand the picture. Da Vinci made certain decisions when painting *The Mona Lisa*, and we will not gain an understanding of the painting until we ask why he made those decisions.

Sister Wendy Beckett, a Catholic nun, gives a fascinating commentary on *The Mona Lisa*. Her take on the picture is that the woman is actually laughing at Da Vinci. Da Vinci is trying to "capture" her, but she knows he is far from understanding the mystery of who she is. Her expression is one of smug triumph at defeating the great Da Vinci. Da Vinci's genius shows, however, in his ability to capture the expression of the woman even though he did not understand what that expression meant. There are of course many interpretations of this painting. Whether you agree or disagree with Sister Wendy (for the record, I agree) the point is that the *why* questions lead us toward a deeper understanding of the picture.

Beginning to understand *The Mona Lisa* is one thing; understanding the world and the greater universe is another. Although Heidegger never found a solid answer to his question *"Why is there something rather than nothing?"*, asking the why question led him to a deeper understanding of existence. Asking the why question also began Greek philosophy some two-and-a-half thousand years ago when Thales of Miletus (624–546 BCE) sought to understand

---

[3] Da Vinci had a special attachment to this painting and was known to carry it with him when he traveled.

the world around him.[4] As a result of thousands of years of subsequent philosophical thought, the four assumptions—*Ontology*, *Epistemology*, *Axiology* (or *Ethics*) and *Teleology*—emerged as central to understanding reality.

Even if you have never heard of words like Ontology or Epistemology, you already have ideas about these assumptions. Our ideas about the four assumptions are important because these ideas form the foundation for how we understand and live in the world. My hope is that, through reading this book, you will gain a better understanding of the assumptions that have such an important impact on how we live our lives.

During the last episode of the first season of *Lost*, Locke is ensnared by The Island Monster and dragged through the jungle. Jack runs after Locke and heroically prevents him from disappearing down a gigantic spider hole. As Jack struggles to keep Locke above ground, Locke tells Jack that he will be okay and asks Jack to let him go. Later that evening as they walk through the jungle, Jack can no longer fight his bewilderment at Locke's response to immanent death:

"Look, I need for you—I need for you to explain to me what the hell's going on inside your head, John. I need to know why you believe that thing wasn't going to..."

"I believe that I was being tested," says Locke.

"Tested?"

"Yeah, tested, that's why you and I don't see eye-to-eye sometimes, Jack—because you're a man of science."

"Yeah, and what does that make you?"

"Me, well, I'm a man of faith. Do you really think all this is

---

[4] Thales is believed to have predicted an eclipse during a battle between the Medes and Lydians in 585 BCE as recorded by Herodotus. Whether or not he actually predicted the eclipse, this moment is often regarded as the beginning of Greek Philosophy.

an accident—that we, a group of strangers survived, many of us with just superficial injuries? Do you think we crashed on this place by coincidence—especially this place? We were brought here for a purpose, for a reason, all of us. Each one of us was brought here for a reason."

"Brought here? And who brought us here, John?"

"The Island. The Island brought us here. This is no ordinary place; you've seen that, I know you have. But The Island chose you, too, Jack. It's destiny."

Although Jack is often bewildered by Locke, he does not dismiss him as a crazy lunatic. Locke is a challenge. Locke does not just hold abstract theories about The Island: he actually lives them out even when his life is in danger. Locke's assumptions about The Island ultimately determine how he responds to life and death. At a certain point in the story of *Lost,* Jack must also come up with an interpretation of events on The Island. The Island demands an interpretation.

When I set out with Nate on our trip around the US, I was dissatisfied with the answers concerning my existence. I had subconsciously absorbed my culture's answers (or, more precisely, non-answers) without realizing it. Like some of the Losties, I was dissatisfied because these answers seemed inadequate. The answers I had subconsciously absorbed left me wondering why my life really mattered and who I was in the world.

In many ways I felt like Bilbo Baggins, who we will meet in Chapter Three: *Middle Earth and Ontology.* After his first adventure with Gandalf in *The Hobbit,* Bilbo just had to go exploring again.

# CHAPTER 3

## *Middle Earth and Ontology*

"I want to see mountains again, Gandalf—*mountains*; and then find somewhere I can rest," lamented Bilbo as he hastily packed his things for his final journey. After one hundred and eleven years in the Shire, Bilbo had finally made up his mind to leave for good.

"I am old, Gandalf. I don't look it, but I am beginning to

feel it in my heart of hearts. Why, I feel all thin, sort of *stretched*, if you know what I mean: like butter that has been scraped across too much bread. That can't be right. I need a change or something."

It had been sixty-one years since Bilbo saw the mountains and wild country of Middle Earth during his first adventure with Gandalf. Bilbo was never quite the same after. Over the years he became estranged from the Shire and its happenings. Instead of sitting by the fire at Bag-End, Bilbo took to spending long hours in his study and going on walks beyond the realms of the Shire. The Shire lost its luster; his heart yearned to return to the enchanted parts of Middle Earth he encountered on his first adventure.

Bilbo was not always fascinated with Middle Earth. In fact, his first fifty years of existence were uneventful, even for a hobbit, and Bilbo was perfectly content. Things began to change one morning, when Bilbo was standing outside the door of his luxurious hobbit hole, Bag-End. As he was enjoying his after-breakfast smoke, an old man wearing a scarf appeared. Bilbo greeted him with a hearty, "Good morning," and blew out a smoke ring. He had no idea that the old man was the legendary Gandalf the Wizard.

"Very pretty!" said Gandalf. "But I have no time to blow smoke-rings this morning. I am looking for someone to share in an adventure that I am arranging, and it's very difficult to find anyone."

"I should think so—in these parts! We are plain quiet folk and have no use for adventures. Nasty disturbing uncomfortable things! Make you late for dinner! I can't think what anyone sees in them."

Bilbo soon learnt the identity of the old man, but remained

resolute in not joining Gandalf for the adventure. He gave the wizard a token invitation to tea the next day and quickly shut his door. Gandalf, however, decided to take Bilbo up on his invitation, and by scratching a sign on Bilbo's front door, he made Bag-End the meeting centre for thirteen dwarves who were about to join him.

The next day, just before tea-time, Bilbo heard his door-bell ring and suddenly remembered his invitation. Expecting to see only the tall figure of Gandalf, he was instead greeted by a dwarf named Dwalin who walked in as if Bilbo was expecting him. Twelve more dwarves arrived, followed by Gandalf. A nice quiet evening sitting by the fire at Bag-End became a raucous gathering with Bilbo as reluctant host.

For much of the evening Bilbo was frustrated and flummoxed. But after the dishes were washed and put away, the dwarves brought out their instruments and started singing. Bilbo forgot his hard feelings. The Dwarf songs of ancient treasure and lands past the misty mountains had a strange effect on him; they made him forget the Shire, and made his heart yearn to see great mountains and explore deep caverns. He became strangely jealous of the dwarves. When the music stopped, he was so confused about his desires that he had half a mind to hide behind the beer barrels in the cellar.

One thing led to the next and before he could comprehend it, Bilbo was off on an adventure to the Lonely Mountain to slay the dragon Smaug. At times, Bilbo wished he was back by the fire at Bag-End, but the strange desires that arose the night of the unexpected party had taken root. Through his adventure with Gandalf and the dwarves, Bilbo was immersed in parts of Middle Earth he had never known existed. Bilbo lost his fear and suspicion of the world outside the Shire. He developed a love for Middle Earth and the good beings who dwelt in it.

For most of the beings that Bilbo meets, Bilbo is the first hobbit they have set eyes on. Hobbits do not leave the Shire, happy for the most part to ignore and be ignored by the outside world. Through the course of his adventure, Bilbo realizes that the Shire is something of a mystery for others: no one seems to know much about it and no one seems to know what a hobbit is.

For the hobbits of the Shire, the beginning of time occurred when the Fallohide brothers, with a great following of hobbits, crossed the Brandywine River in the one-thousand-six-hundred-and-first year of the Third Age. The crossing of the Brandywine is marked as the *Shire Reckoning*. It marks year one of the Shire, the reference point for dating all happenings in hobbit history. Over time, the hobbits became estranged from outside events and beings. As long as there is peace and quiet, they see no need to venture out and get involved with the outside world.

The hobbits have a vague sense that they are part of a bigger world, but for the most part they are happy to be isolated. Through the course of his adventure, however, Bilbo learns that the story of the Shire is a mere footnote in the elaborate history of Middle Earth. Through his adventure, during which he is transformed from a reluctant companion to something of a hero, Bilbo's knowledge of Middle Earth deepens. He becomes more familiar with its elaborate history; further, he develops a more accurate idea of the *nature of reality* in Middle Earth.

Another word used to describe the nature of reality is *On-

*tology*, the first peak of our imagined philosophical mountain range. Ontology is derived from the Greek words *ontos* (οντος) and *logos* (λογος)—*ontos* is a Greek participle which means *being*. *Logos* in this instance means discourse. Ontology deals with the question, *what does it mean to be*? From the perspective of Bilbo Baggins, Ontology deals with the question, what does it mean to be a hobbit on Middle Earth?

What it means to *be* is a profound and important question. Although Ontology focuses on what it *means to be*, it ultimately derives from our assumptions about the *nature of reality*. As humans we are all in reality but, as we shall see in this chapter, we all *interpret* reality. The nature of reality does not change according to our interpretation, but how we interpret reality will determine how we see ourselves in that reality.

Bilbo's idea of what it means to be a hobbit changes because Bilbo changes his ideas about the nature of reality. Prior to his first adventure he is fearful and suspicious about other beings in Middle Earth, but through his adventures he discovers that he enjoys the company of dwarves, elves and wizards. Bilbo wondered why anyone would leave the Shire, but when he returns all he wants to do is go exploring once more.

Bilbo encounters new places and beings on his adventure, but he also begins to see the special ways in which Middle Earth works which were not visible to him in the Shire. Bilbo encounters various objects and beings—a magical ring, an enchanted forest, an ancient dragon. As well as seeing the magic and enchantment, Bilbo discerns that Middle Earth is caught in an ongoing battle between light and darkness. Good beings are attracted to the light;

some even emanate it. Evil beings are repelled by the light. Light is not just a physical wave in Bilbo's world; it manifests itself in the beings of Middle Earth.

The mysterious and magical way that his world works is a constant wonder to Bilbo, and it forces him to rethink what it means to be a hobbit in Middle Earth. The new and different things Bilbo sees cause him to ask the *what* question about beings such as elves and goblins, which inevitably leads him to the *why* question.

As we saw in Chapter Two with the Mona Lisa illustration, we cannot understand what is there until we ask *why* it is there. The *what* question arouses Bilbo's curiosity, but the *why* question ultimately enables him to understand Middle Earth and its beings. Although Bilbo can never fully comprehend the nature of reality on Middle Earth, his understanding of Middle Earth improves through asking the why question.

In the sixty-one years after his first adventure, Bilbo lives a very different life. His prior ideas about Middle Earth change dramatically and he is forced to reevaluate who he is in relation to the new and exciting world he now perceives. Bilbo still lives at Bag-End, drinks ale and smokes pipe-weed, but the way he views his existence and lives his life is fundamentally different.

Although my adventures with Nate in The Bus were no match for the drama of Bilbo's adventure through Middle Earth, my existence after that trip differed greatly from the life I lived before. I still lived in a dorm room at State College, drank lots of Mountain Dew during exams, and went to lectures, but the way I understood my existence was different. The nature of reality at State College didn't change during the summer of '96, but my *in-*

*terpretation* of that reality did. I answered the *what* questions about my existence in a way similar to that before I left, but I began changing my answers to the *why* questions.

Through the course of this chapter you will see that through history, Westerners have had different interpretations of reality. These changes are best illustrated through variation in the arts. Artists have always painted people and objects, but large movements in art history are ultimately driven by gradually-changing views on the nature of reality and consequent changes in how artists understand their own existence. Again, the nature of reality hasn't changed throughout Western history, but people's *interpretation* of that reality has.

How we interpret reality is important because this ultimately influences how we understand our existence and what it means to "be". In the same way that Bilbo's new understanding of Middle Earth changed his ideas of what it meant to be a hobbit, the way we understand reality influences how we understand ourselves as humans. Throughout this chapter you will see that changing interpretations of reality through history carries through to influence how Westerners understand themselves as humans—what is known today as *anthropology*.

Today most people believe that as humans we have progressed in our interpretation of reality through history in the same way that technology has progressed. The problem with this belief is that no commonly-held view or interpretation of the nature of reality exists in the West today. We understand ourselves to be in the *Postmodern Age* but *Postmodernism* does not actually represent a particular understanding of reality or existence. *Postmodernism* rather represents confusion and doubt about the nature of reality, a confusion reflected in the art of our time.

Although we live in the *Postmodern Age,* we continue to hold ideas about our existence and the nature of reality. It is simply impossible to live this life without forming ideas about the nature of reality and what it means to be human. Whether we believe that everything came from the Big Bang and we evolved from simpler animals or that we descended from Adam and Eve, we all interpret our reality to a certain extent and attempt to provide ourselves with answers to questions about our existence.

Perhaps the biggest question we all inevitably face is: *How do we know that we have interpreted reality correctly?* Bilbo spent his first fifty years believing an elementary and often *incorrect* interpretation of Middle Earth. Bilbo assumed the other hobbits were right in their interpretation of Middle Earth. Only through his adventure did his ideas begin to change.

Ontology deals with the issue of "what it means to be" but a more accurate definition of Ontology is *one's own interpretation of reality.* One's interpretation of reality determines what it means to be in reality. Ontology is an important term, but it can be misleading because it does not refer to reality itself but to the interpretation that we all make of reality. *The nature of reality,* or more precisely *one's interpretation of the nature of reality,* is more helpful; this indicates both the process of interpretation behind the term Ontology and what is being interpreted. In this chapter I will use the word "Ontology", but when I do remember that it is defined as one's (or humans) interpretation of reality.

I will say more about the process of interpretation in Chapter Five, on *Epistemology*; there, through the agency of a mysterious button that the Losties find on The Island, we will explore the nature of *knowledge* and how it is that we can know things. In Chapter Seven, on *Ethics,* I will explore how humans act in reality, with a focus on human sexuality. In Chapter Nine I will discuss *Teleology*, the end or purpose of things, with a focus on the *telos* or purpose of human beings. And in Chapter Eleven, on *The Hope of Redemption,* I will look at why humans can legitimately hope to live up to their potential.

A lot of ground will be covered in this book, and in the course of reading you will be led through several thousand years of thought about our existence. For many people the ground that I cover will be basic revision; for others, it will be new. I have tried to make things easy to understand but depending on the reader's educational background there may be difficulties in comprehension.

Although things do get complicated I believe, as I said in Chapter Two, that it is possible for the "man (or woman) on the street" to understand what I am saying. My motivation in saying complex things is not to make myself appear more intelligent; rather, questions concerning our existence are by nature complex. If you persist through the hard parts of this book, you will be duly rewarded.

As we progress through the philosophical mountain range the going will get tough. At times you might find you want to go and make yourself a hot drink midway through a chapter. There is nothing wrong with taking a break to reflect on what you have read. In fact this is probably the best way to read. I can't promise you an easy time, but I can promise that as we progress the climbing gets easier—even fun.

Along the way, we will follow the ongoing adventures of Nate and myself. These chapters provide some level of relief (and hopefully entertainment), but they are also connected to the larger journey. If there is one thing that you learn from reading, let it be that abstract ideas discussed in the academy and university philosophy departments end up meeting all of us in the here and now.

The first mountain, Ontology, is probably the most difficult. Take your time and don't feel that you need to understand everything in order to progress—just keep moving. Matters will eventually become clear. Throughout this climb we will spend time at various philosopher's cabins, particularly Plato and Aristotle, and we will go over a portion of Western history beginning with the Greeks.

## The Greeks

In today's modern world, it is hard to think of the sun as an object physically moved across the sky by the actions of a god. It is hard to comprehend that appeasing certain gods could be thought to influence rainfall, the growth of grain, the protection of a man's house and pasture, and the outcome of battles, but it is from this world view, that of the Greeks, that the West was born.

The gods played a central part in how the Greeks lived and understood themselves as humans. The Greeks who lived during the archaic age (roughly twelfth to ninth century BCE) and classic age (eighth century onwards) all believed in the existence of gods;

these gods exerted an important influence over their daily existence, directing almost every area of life, from earthquakes (Poseidon) to the waves of the ocean (Amphitrite). Although Greek epics and poetry were often fictional, the perceived role of Greek gods in everyday life is accurately portrayed in epics like *The Iliad* and *The Odyssey*.

Thales of Miletus (624–546 BCE) is considered the father of Greek philosophy. Thales and other thinkers after him were part of the Ionian enlightenment, centered at Miletus in modern-day Turkey. Ionian enlightenment thinkers speculated on the nature of reality, science, and other questions. Important thinkers after Thales included Parmenides (520-450 BCE), Anaxagoras (500-428 BCE), and Protagoras (490-420 BCE). The reason why Thales and other thinkers began to speculate on these philosophical issues remains a mystery; regardless, they began a movement of ideas which developed through time and continues up to the present day.

Thales and his compatriots, however, all stand in the shadow of a man who came after them: Socrates (469-399 BCE). Socrates is so important to Greek philosophy that his life is considered a juncture point in Greek thought; philosophers before Socrates are known as pre-Socratics and those after him are called post-Socratics. Socrates' mission in life was to find wisdom; he traveled from city to city looking for anybody considered wise.

## Socrates

In the course of his travels Socrates had many conversations with famous teachers and so-called wise men. More often than not they stormed off in anger after conversing with him. The thoughts of Socrates were so profound and disturbing to the Athenian establishment that he was labeled a disturber of the peace and put on trial for corrupting young people and teaching against the gods. Socrates was given the chance to live, but this decision was conditional on him stopping his teaching activities. Socrates could not abandon his search for truth and chose to die by drinking hemlock.

In Socrates' numerous conversations with other people, he realized that they used words they could not define, such as "beauty" and "justice". People he talked to had ideas about what these words referenced, but whenever Socrates asked people to define them they were left tongue-tied. Socrates wasn't sure himself what the words meant, and this led his student, Plato (428–348 BCE), to formulate the *world of forms*: a world beyond the seen world.[1]

The unseen world of forms was different from the world of Greek gods. It was believed to be the ultimate source of ideas or *universals,* which seemed to repeat themselves in various arenas of reality. These universals included justice and beauty and things such as shapes, colors, and numbers. Whilst the world of the gods was in constant turmoil and variation, Plato's world of unseen forms was ordered, unified, and constant.

The concept of the unseen world of forms changed the course of Western philosophy. Concepts such as *beauty* and *justice* were not foreign to pre-Socratics, but they were not the subject of serious philosophical inquiry. Philosophers prior to Socrates focused mainly on the visible rather than examining what lay behind the material world. The thought of Socrates and Plato led philoso-

---

[1] It can be hard to tell whether Plato simply borrowed ideas from Socrates or whether he developed Socrates' ideas. We mostly have Socrates' dialogues recorded by Plato which are not a systematic representation of Socrates' thought. By and large, Plato is believed to have carried on the thought of Socrates and further developed his ideas.

phy beyond the physical world of substance to the unseen world of forms.

Platonic thought about this unseen world developed (especially through his student Aristotle) and came to be known in the medieval university as *Metaphysics* . The word *Metaphysics* is important because it is the term that *Ontology* replaced in the seventeenth century. This change in terminology was far from cosmetic. Rather, it represents a critical juncture in interpretation of the nature of reality, which I will discuss in detail in Chapter Five.

Bilbo was no stranger to unseen realities during his first adventure. Indeed, Bilbo enters the unseen world himself through the agency of a magical ring he finds in the Misty Mountains. Bilbo also experiences the unseen power of the enchanted Mirkwood Forest and uses his magical ring to rescue his traveling companions from peril. No philosophers in the Shire were contemplating unseen realities during Bilbo's time, which made Bilbo the first hobbit to deal with them. Unfortunately for Bilbo, there were no hobbit equivalents of Plato to help him, whose cabin we shall stop by now.

## Plato

A humble bicycle wheel is a good way to begin understanding the thought of Plato. The centre or hub of the wheel represents the *Demiurge* or God-figure, unifying the wheel and centering the spokes. Those spokes, which emanate from the centre, can be thought of as the world of forms. All of the forms are centered around the *Demiurge* and they all move towards the *good,* the direction of the wheel's rotation.

If the bicycle hub and spokes represents the unseen world, the circumference of the wheel represents the seen world of actual objects or the world of *substance*. In Plato's system, the unseen world of forms, represented by the hub and spokes, somehow connects or passes through the seen world represented by the wheel's rim. In this way Plato believed that objects could be understood as having two causes: *formal* and *material*.[2]

In the case of a table, the *formal cause* has to do with the object's shape or *form*. Plato believed that in the world of forms there resides an ideal table which somehow exists in every physical table. The *formal cause* of every table is thus the ideal table. The *material cause* has to do with the seen world and accounts for the physical substance of the table. In this case, the material cause is some kind of wood and the formal and material causes are the things of which the table consists.

Plato's theory of forms helped solve some of Socrates' riddles, but it created other conundrums. Plato held that forms were separate, but there are numerous instances in which forms seem to combine within particular objects in the visible world. A human being would be a form for Plato, but characteristic of a human being are other forms like colors, such as blue eyes, and legs, which are also seen in tables. Further still, human beings tend to move themselves rather than being moved solely by the *Demiurge*.

Plato's idea worked well with concepts like beauty and justice, which are in a sense unseen and intangible. When it came to explaining forms which have a physical existence in particular objects, however, Plato faced serious challenges. He was not particu-

---

[2] Plato himself would not have affirmed a material cause for objects because he didn't actually believe the seen world counted as knowledge. But in his philosophical discussion he did refer to material objects—a tension in his philosophical system.

larly concerned with physical objects, as the predominant Greek view of reality held that the material world was of less consequence or value than the world of the gods (this view explains why the gods were so prominent in Greek culture). In the thought of Plato, the unseen world of forms held more importance than the seen world of substance.

It is because of Plato's emphasis on forms that a *gap* or *discontinuity* developed between the unseen world and the physical world. Somehow the unseen forms meshed with the seen world, but he wasn't able to explain how the invisible spokes of the wheel meshed with seen physical objects. He also wasn't able to explain how the unseen forms seemed to integrate in seen objects or account for the particular motion of those objects. Plato was well aware of this weakness in his philosophical system. One of his theories suggested that the spokes of the wheel splayed into even more particular elements, which eventually connected with the material world. Despite Plato's best efforts, however, he wasn't able to sufficiently explain how the unseen forms integrated with the seen world.

Plato's understanding of the nature of reality also influenced his thought about the nature of human beings. Plato was not that interested in physical objects: thus, he was not that interested in the human body. For Plato, the human soul or spirit was most important. He viewed humans as souls trapped in a bodily cage. As a result, the course of our earthly life held less consequence than the life of the spirit and engaging in philosophical wisdom.

## Aristotle

The next philosopher we will meet as we move up the mountain of Ontology is Aristotle, Plato's greatest student. The problem with great students, however, is that they tend to oppose their great teachers, sometimes even surpassing them and writing books which oppose them. Aristotle disagreed with Plato on some important matters, but he was also influenced by his teacher in ways that Aristotle himself may not have realized.

Aristotle is important because his thought largely formed the foundations for the scientific revolution in the seventeenth century. As we shall see in Chapter Five, Newton, Boyle, and other thinkers would not have made their discoveries without the thought of Aristotle. Aristotle is somewhat harder to understand than Plato, and for this reason Plato was more popular than Aristotle among the Roman Empire's elite. Although Plato was more immediately comprehensible, in many ways Aristotle's thought surpassed him.

Instead of focusing on unseen forms, Aristotle focused on particular objects and their motion or change. The reference point for understanding reality for Aristotle was individual objects and how they moved. Aristotle dispensed with Plato's separate world of forms and replaced them with another unseen world of *prime matter*.

The world of prime matter is the subject of Aristotle's *Metaphysics,* which he considered the first science and that most central to understanding reality. Metaphysics, which literally means "beyond physics", is derived from the Greek words *meta* and *fusika* (μετά φυσικά) which together mean "beyond what is."[3] For Aristotle, metaphysics held preeminence because it dealt with what lay beyond the physical world. Aristotle wrote a great deal about the physical world, such as *Physics* and *The History of Animals,* but *Metaphysics* is specifically about the unseen. Aristotle observed that all objects are in motion and set about explaining that movement. Questions such as what made a plant grow or what caused the motion of a stone as it was thrown through the air drove his work.

While Plato only affirmed two causes—the *material* and the *formal*—Aristotle added two more: the *efficient* cause and the *final* cause. The *efficient* cause is what brought the table into existence: a carpenter. The *final cause* is the end for which the table was made: a dining room table for a family. If we think about a stone moving through the air, the *formal cause* is a stone and the *material cause* is some kind of rock material. The *efficient cause* is the original cause of motion and the *final cause* is where the stone will land. Aristotle suggested that each physical object had a corresponding *essence* unique to that object which gave the object its form and caused it to move.

A modern parallel of this idea can be seen in the film *The Matrix* (1999). In the world of the Matrix, all objects are programs run by a central computer. The objects are real to those in the Matrix, but what is actually most real is the programming code which gives each object its form and motion. In the same way that programming code is most real in the Matrix, Aristotle considered *prime matter* or *essence* most real in his philosophical system.

It is unseen prime matter or essence which scientists are

---

[3] In Greek φυσικά (from which we get the word "physics") literally means "the natural created order of things."

trying to identify today using particle colliders. Although Newton formulated his theory of gravitation almost four hundred years ago, scientists still don't know why masses are attracted to one another. Gravity explains the *result* of the attraction between masses, but it does not explain *why* the inherent attraction between masses exists. It is because of this inconsistency that scientists know "The Higgs Particle" must somehow exist within matter. I will say more about the world of essence or prime matter in Chapter Five, but the main point here is that Aristotle considered the world of essence central to understanding reality.

Aristotle in a sense reinvented Plato's wheel. Imagine that instead of the bicycle wheel of Plato we now have an elaborate system of gears. Instead of a separate unseen world of forms, the seen and unseen world are integrated in each gear. Each gear has an associated unseen element, called *essence*, which is like the programming code behind what is seen. Aristotle's gear system resembles that of a complex watch; the central drive wheel is the *Unmoved Mover* who initially moved the mechanism. Like Plato, Aristotle believed in an invisible centre of reality. However, he affirms it as an impersonal *Unmoved Mover* rather than Plato's more personal *Demiurge*.

Aristotle's system necessitated an *Unmoved Mover*, as everything had an efficient cause. In the case of the table, its *efficient cause* is the carpenter. But what is the *efficient cause* of the carpenter? The carpenter descended from his parents, but how far back does his genealogical line go? Causes could not go back ad infinitum; at some point things had to begin to move or change. The solution was an *Unmoved Mover*, a force that began motion but was itself *uncaused* or *unmoved*. Aristotle wasn't sure if there was just one Unmoved Mover or several unified Unmoved Movers, but this entity ultimately began all motion.

Aristotle solved a number of problems with his new system. In particular, he fixed the discontinuity between the seen and unseen worlds by integrating them. Each physical object had a corresponding essence which gave the object its form and motion. Aristotle also fixed Plato's forms problem by suggesting that the forms were not universal and separate but were built into the essence of each object.

The gear system of Aristotle was not like a precisely engineered Swiss watch, however—it was more like a *magical watch*. Rather than a precise, synchronized *mechanical watch*, the gears somehow turned themselves; it wasn't easy to predict what each gear would do. The motion of the whole system was connected, but each of the gears had a life of its own. The watch worked and told the time, but Aristotle did not know exactly how this result was achieved.

In regard to planets or heavenly bodies, Aristotle believed these entities occupied a different realm of reality. Consequently, their motion was beyond human explanation. Aristotle had not conceived of universal invisible forces, such as gravitation or the transference of momentum, which today we know are crucial to plotting the course of a stone thrown through the air. The preciseness with which physicists like Newton could predict the motion of the planets and projectiles would have been mere fantasy in Aristotle's world.

The genius of Aristotle's system was that he decentralized

the world of forms and integrated them into the *essence* (or prime matter) of each individual object. Forms did not dominate Aristotle's system like they did Plato's. But the genius of Aristotle's system was also its weakness: it was difficult to unify. Aristotle held that each gear in the magical watch had an individual essence. Yet, certain gears looked and behaved similarly to others. In fact, there were remarkable similarities between whole groups of gears; this seemed to suggest a distinct relation and sharing of the essences Aristotle insisted were separate. This unity or sameness in reality led Plato to imagine the unseen forms. In insisting on the separateness of things, Aristotle had trouble explaining apparent unities.

In solving the problem created by Plato, then, Aristotle inadvertently caused another: resolving the tension between separateness and unity. This riddle confounded thinkers for centuries to come. It would be another fifteen hundred years before Thomas Aquinas (1225-1274 CE) made progress on resolving this tension. Although Aristotle was not able to resolve the unity problem, he solved a vital problem with Plato's system—the disconnect between the seen and unseen worlds.

Because Aristotle believed that objects were moved by causes rather than the gods, his thought tended to diminish the influence of the Greek gods. But Aristotle's thought did not go mainstream; most Greeks held true to the belief that the gods moved reality. The Athenian academies run by philosophers like Plato and Aristotle were not institutions like universities today; their influence on mainstream culture was minor. Greek boys and girls were not educated like most kids today; rather, education was for society's elite. Subsequently the view of unseen Greek gods dominating life persisted.

## The Romans

The Greek empire (under Macedonia) reached its peak under Aristotle's student, Alexander the Great (356-323 BCE), and was eventually swallowed up by the Roman Empire during the second century BCE. Although the Romans incorporated much of Greek culture into their own, they did not make many advances on Greek philosophy. The Roman Empire was founded on military power and economics, not education. Views on the nature of reality in the Roman Empire were thus similar to those of the Greeks and remained fairly constant throughout Rome's early history.

An important juncture in the Western view of reality is the conversion of the Roman Emperor Constantine (272–337 CE). Constantine's conversion, believed to have been caused by the Christian God, helped him win the battle of Milvian Bridge in 312 CE. Before the battle, Constantine looked up into the sky and saw a sign of the Cross accompanied by the words, "By this, conquer."

Despite centuries of persecution, Christianity already had an established base among common people, including Constantine's mother, at the time of Constantine's conversion. It is believed that Constantine's conversion caused more converts than any other human being's.[4] Constantine legalized Christianity in the Roman Empire with the Edict of Milan in 313 CE, and this culminated in Christianity becoming the state religion in 356 CE when the Christian Roman Emperor Constantius II issued a decree closing all pagan temples.[5]

---

[4] Jaroslav Pelikan, *Acts, Brazos Commentary Series* (Grand Rapids: Brazos Press, 2005): 267, quoted in John Meyendorff, *Imperial Unity and Christian Divisions* (Crestwood: St. Vladimir's Press, 1989), 6-7.

[5] Christianity was decriminalized in 313 CE by the Edict of Milan rather than being made the official religion of the Roman Empire, but the Edict of Milan was *interpreted* as making Christianity the official religion of the Empire.

The view of reality implicit in Christianity was entirely different from that of the Romans. According to the Book of Genesis, the first book of the Old Testament (known as the Tanakh by Jews), God created the world and everything in it. God made the world perfect, but the first two humans, Adam and Eve, ate fruit from the Tree of Knowledge of Good and Evil, causing themselves and all of creation to be corrupted. This episode is known as the fall.

God wished to restore his creation, however, and for this purpose he chose Abraham to found the nation of Israel. In time, this would bless all nations and ultimately bring redemption to all creation. Christians believe that Jesus of Nazareth (4 BCE – 29 CE), born of the Virgin Mary, began a new age of redemption for the world. Jesus was the Christ or Messiah of which the Old Testament spoke; he was God and man simultaneously, a person of the Holy Trinity, which consisted of God the Father, God the Son (Jesus Christ), and the Holy Spirit. The doctrine of the Trinity, so essential to the Christian faith, dictated in its most simple form God was one and three at the same time.

According to Christian belief, there were *no* gods except the Triune God. Worshipping false gods was a sin. As a result, pagan temples were destroyed and replaced by churches; later, temples in the Roman Forum were also converted to churches. Paganism had strong roots in the Roman Empire, however, and continued to be a part of Roman culture. Yet Christianity ultimately surpassed it as the dominant religion.

Unlike the Greeks (including Aristotle), who believed that the world was eternal, early Christians believed God created everything, including matter, and that all he made was good. Consequently, Christians had a higher view of matter than pagans; in particular, they held a higher view of human beings. Unlike the Romans, who only considered Roman citizens valuable, Christians believed *all* human beings were created in God's image. The increased value of the individual led to the formation of hospitals, monasteries, and other institutions to serve those society had formerly cast off. When the Western Roman Empire crumbled in the fifth century, these institutions and the church became the glue that held the West together.

## Augustine

The Western Roman Empire's collapse was a cataclysmic event. Many Romans put the blame at the feet of Christianity (due to the Romans' view that the gods determined history). Many Romans believed that Rome's abandonment of the pagan gods caused the empire to fall. In response to this charge Augustine of Hippo (354–430 CE) wrote a defense of Christianity called *The City of God*. Augustine, whose writings influenced the West for more than a millenia, is important to the story of Ontology, and we will now spend some time conversing at his cabin.

Because Plato's thought was an important step in his conversion, Augustine was influenced by Plato's view of reality. For most Christian theologians of the West and East, Plato's thought was more attractive because his *Demiurge* was more personal than Aristotle's removed *Unmoved Mover* (Plato's works were also easier to understand).

Plato's theory of forms became Augustine's *doctrine of universals*, which remained prevalent in Western thought; it featured in the work of thinkers as late as the English philosopher John Locke (1632-1704). While Plato's *Demiurge* was attractive, the implicit problems in his philosophy carried through to people's view of reality. Augustine inherited the gap problem from Plato, separating the seen and unseen worlds and thus emphasizing the unseen world at the expense of the seen. Augustine had a higher view of the material world than Plato because he believed that God did make everything and called it good, but the material world was always lesser.

## Transition to The Medieval Age

With the siege of Hippo by the Vandals in 430 CE, Augustine witnessed first hand the collapse of the Western Roman Empire. The Eastern Roman Empire, known as Byzantium, continued on for another thousand years. Byzantium was the name of the town that Constantine renamed Constantinople (modern-day Istanbul) and made the new capital of the Empire, in 330 CE, under direction from the Christian God. In the West, various reincarnations of the Holy Roman Empire began in 800 CE under Charlemagne (742-814 CE) and lasted until 1806. Historians have jested, however, that the various incarnations were not holy, not Roman, and certainly not empires.

The instability of the West after the first sack of Rome in 410 CE and the subsequent period of economic and intellectual decline contributed to Aristotle falling out of circulation. The West and East were already divided by language (Latin in the West; Greek in the East). Over time they also developed different theological traditions. This was due to geographic separation [John of Damascus (676-749 CE), one of the greatest Eastern theologians, never heard of Augustine] but was also due to Aristotle's thought somehow getting lost in the West.

Eastern Theologians had access to Plato, but they also had access to Aristotle. In many regards Aristotle surpassed Plato's thought. This accessibility is evident in the writings of Gregory of Nazianzus (329-390 CE), Gregory of Nyssa (335-394 CE) and John of Damascus (676-749 CE), as seen in *An Exact Exposition of the Orthodox Faith*. The Greek theologians replaced Aristotle's Unmoved Mover with the God of the scriptures and linked God with the makeup of the seen world.

Because Aristotle assumed that matter was eternal and was primarily interested in the motion of things, he did not speculate much on how humans came into existence or on their physical appearance. The Greek fathers, however, believed that God specifically and intentionally created humans and that human beings were the crowning achievement of his creation. The Eastern theologians viewed the created world as a *second book* which, following the Holy Scriptures, revealed the nature of God. Given the intentionality of creation, the Greek Fathers focused on questions like why God made man walk upright.

Although most of the Eastern theologians favored Aristotle, Pseudo-Dionysius the Areopagite, a Syrian thinker in the sixth century, was an exception. In his book, *On the Divine Names,* Pseudo-Dionysius introduced the concept of *divine processions* or *energies* from God; these closely resembled Plato's world of forms. These processions are the names of God which appear in the scriptures, such as Light, Spirit, Fire, Love, Wisdom, Righteousness, Holiness, and Beauty. Pseudo-Dionysius' thought influenced Thomas Aquinas, who would make the first serious attempt to resolve the unity problem in Aristotle's thought. Before I get to Aquinas (a Western theologian), however, it is important to understand how the thought of Aristotle found its way back into the West after being lost for hundreds of years.

## The Rise of Islam

In the year 632 CE the Arabs began to unify under the prophet Muhammad (570-632 CE). The Arabs were largely forgotten by the Roman and Persian Empires, but by the end of the seventh century they had conquered many former Roman territories and were knocking on the door of Western Europe. The Byzantine Empire was challenged throughout its history, but Islam was its biggest test. By the seventh century the Byzantine Empire had lost Jerusalem, Damascus, Antioch, and large regions of North Africa. In the space of a few hundred years, much of the East found itself under enforced Islam.[6]

Charles Martel (688-741 CE) and the Franks finally stopped the advance of the Islamic Moors in the West at the Battle of Tours in 732 CE, while Byzantium held off invasion from Islamic armies in the East until Constantinople fell in 1453 to the Ottoman Empire. The Islamic invasions and corresponding crusades resulted in the deaths of millions and were a disaster for humanity,

---

[6] Monophysites and Nestorians willingly embraced Islam as a liberator.

but a by-product of the wreckage was that the learning of the Arabs, including the thought of Aristotle, came back into circulation in the West.[7]

As a result of the crusades, Christians and Muslims found themselves in close proximity after the capture of Toledo in 1085 (in modern-day Spain) and the Norman conquest of Southern Italy and Sicily in the eleventh century. The interaction between Muslims and Christians was especially prominent in Toledo; they learnt each other's language and exchanged knowledge.[8]

This sharing of intellectual wealth between Christians and Muslims was most beneficial for Western Christians, however. From the fall of the Roman Empire until the eleventh century, the West was in steady intellectual decline, trailing the Arab world in almost all areas of learning—science, medicine, astronomy, mathematics. Westerners borrowed from the Arabs in all of these areas, and it was in places like Toledo and Sicily that they finally stumbled upon Arabic translations of Aristotle.[9]

Even though manuscripts of Aristotle were abundant in the East, none of them had been translated into Latin. As a result the West proceeded largely as if Aristotle had never existed.[10] Arabic translations of Aristotle stirred great excitement in Western scholars; they enthusiastically translated Aristotle into Latin during the eleventh and twelfth centuries. This frenzy of translation resulted in a massive influx of Aristotle's thought into the West.

At the same time Aristotle was being reintroduced, learning centers called universities began to arise for the first time in the history of human civilization. The term "university" was derived from the Latin term *universitas*, which meant community or corpo-

---

[7] Renewed contact with Eastern Christians led to Aristotle being encountered in the original Greek. Robert Grosseteste (1175-1253) of Oxford made early translations directly from these sources.
[8] Edward Grant, *Foundations of Modern Science in the Middle Ages* (Cambridge: Cambridge University Press, 2007), 24-25..
[9] Ibid., 18-19.
[10] The Western theologian Boethius (480-524 CE) is an exception.

ration and was originally used to describe guilds. Universities are important to the story of Ontology because they became the nerve centre of ideas—including ideas about the nature of reality—in the West.

In the Shire, at the time of Bilbo, there were no universities or even libraries. Little hobbit children did not go to schools or universities. Gandalf was able to access large libraries through the various wizard schools on Middle Earth, but the hobbits of the Shire had no such resources. During the fourth age, Frodo and Bilbo's writings demonstrated the value of reading and libraries began to appear in the Shire. Like libraries in the Shire, universities have not always been with us in the West. Due to their continued importance, it is necessary to give a brief description of their origins.[11]

## The Medieval University

After hundreds of years of instability, by the eleventh century Western Europe had stabilized. By the end of the twelfth century, European commerce and manufacturing was greater than at the height of the Roman Empire. Increased commercial life in urban centers gave rise to guilds, in which people from like trades could gather and share knowledge. The different guilds realized they could benefit from such exchanges, and associations formed. Political leaders also realized the benefit of association and gave guild members legal status.

Schools of theology, medicine, and the arts, operating individually and informally at the time, observed the advantages of

---

[11] For a fuller description see Chapter Three of Edward Grant's book, *The Foundations of Modern Science in the Middle Ages* (Cambridge: Cambridge University Press, 2007).

guild association. These schools had struggled because the state authorities did not recognize them or give them any privileges. The success of association in sharing and developing knowledge encouraged teaching masters and students to form their own legal corporations or universities. The name *studium generale* was used to refer to large schools in Paris, Oxford, and Bologna. These learning centers featured at least three of the four traditional faculties (arts, theology, law, medicine), a condition of the name *studium generale*. *Studium generale* is what we know today as the modern university.

Universities shared knowledge and ideas cooperatively, enabling ideas to travel across geographic boundaries. The formation of universities institutionalized education and the increasing number of universities and students enabled the thought of an individual to have a major influence on the surrounding culture.

## Thomas Aquinas

Because Aristotle's thought was on the rise at the time universities began to form, his influence on the medieval university was profound. Westerners still held a Christian view of reality, but their ideas were largely shaped by Plato (due to the influence of Augustine), not Aristotle. Aristotle was thus viewed as a threat by the Christian establishment. Such was his influence that Western theologians had to deal with the apparent and real conflicts between their theology and Aristotelian thought. The man to take on this challenge was Thomas Aquinas (1225–1274 CE), whose cabin we will stop at now.

Aquinas was the intellectual giant of his time and remains so in Catholic theology today. Aquinas was influenced by Eastern theologians such as John of Damascus and Gregory Nazianzus, but he was also influenced by Pseudo-Dionysius' doctrine of the divine names. The biggest influence on Aquinas, however, was Aristotle, whom he called "the philosopher."

Aquinas disagreed with Aristotle on issues such as the origin of matter and Aristotle's impersonal Unmoved Mover, but set himself to solve the unity problem nonetheless. The unity problem was particularly pressing because, as a Christian, Aquinas believed that the Triune God of the scriptures created everything and held all things together. If one God ordered the whole universe, the disunity in Aristotle's system needed to be addressed.

Aquinas' answer to Aristotle's ancient riddle was his doctrine of *Analogy*. Aquinas, like Aristotle, believed in distinct essences, but Aquinas also saw truth in the *divine names* of Pseudo-Dionysius. Whilst Aquinas believed that the seen forms or universals, such as colors and shapes, existed in the mind of God, he believed divine energies like Love, Wisdom, Righteousness, and Beauty had a real existence, universally, within creation.

Aquinas often uses the example of health to explain Analogy. Health is not a definable entity, but it is evident in a creature like a parrot that has a healthy-looking plume, a well-proportioned body, and moves well. But health is also present in the food that the parrot eats, which is vital to the parrot being healthy. Aquinas' point is that, while health is difficult to define, it has a real existence that takes on different forms in different objects. Ultimately, it unifies those objects.

Aquinas' doctrine of Analogy argued that living beings shared in divine forms such as health and beauty. In this way individuals were also unified. Aquinas believed that due to the varying presence of divine forms, there were degrees or rankings of being. God was the ultimate expression of being because he was the source of the divine forms which percolated down to various beings on Earth; humans in turn were the highest of beings on Earth. God was not just a super-being, however. God was in essence unfathomable and beyond human thought. The world God created did reveal something of what he was like because its beings were unified and participated in the divine forms. The beings of the world were like or *analogous* to one another because they shared in the divine forms.

## The Medieval Age

The thought of Aristotle influenced theologians such as Aquinas, Francis of Assisi (1182-1226), Bonaventure (1221-1274), and the Italian poet Dante (1265-1321). The Medieval Age stood in the shadow of Aristotle for the next four hundred years. Prior to the influx of Aristotle's thought, the gap between the unseen world and seen world led to the belief that humans could not know or understand the motion of things. This was due to the gap or discontinuity in Plato's system and to lingering ideas from paganism, where gods moved things unpredictably.

The thought of Aristotle, combined with Christian ideas

about God, led to the belief that God could be known through how things looked—and how they *moved*. Aristotle assumed crucially that the motion of things *could* be explained. His explanations of motion in the *Physics* might seem primitive today, but permeating his thought was the vital assumption that motion could be explained.

Influenced by Aristotle's thought, the thinkers of the Medieval Age believed the motion of objects in the world did not present unsolvable mysteries. Rather, God caused motion and through seeing how things moved, the God who causes them to move could be understood. God revealed himself through the scriptures, known as *special revelation*, and through his creation, known as *general revelation*. I will say more about this in Chapter Five.

The fear and superstition that prevented medieval humans from going out and exploring the world began to be replaced by wonder and excitement. By seeing how the world worked, one could know more about the God who designed it. Similarly, by studying the nature of God in the scriptures or theology, humans could know more about the motion of objects. Man began to climb mountains and explore the world with increased vigor.

This sense of wonder transferred through to God himself. As the West continued its economic rise, large cathedrals were built in cities such as Paris (begun in 1163), York (begun in 1220), Cologne (begun in 1248), and Milan (begun in 1386). Some took hundreds of years to build. The architecture of the cathedrals reflected key elements of the Christian faith and the heavenly realm of saints and angels towards which man was ultimately headed.

Medievals were in God's world. They understood themselves to be created and loved by God as revealed through the Holy Scriptures and the coming of Christ in the flesh.

Medievals were a long way from opening science labs, however, because the way things moved still mystified them. The medievals held a *magical ontological watch* idea of motion rather than the engineered Swiss watch of Kepler (1571-1630) or Newton (1643-1727). Nevertheless, a newfound interest in the world and how things moved was born.

The study of how things moved became known as *Natural Philosophy,* which became a serious discipline in the medieval university. Theology and Natural Philosophy were frequently taught at the same university, and there were often tensions between the disciplines. By and large natural philosophy sided with Aristotle in almost all areas; this led to conflicts with theology over such topics as the origin of matter or the nature of God. Theology was the queen of the sciences, however, and held sway, but the natural philosophers subtly undercut the authority of the school of theology in their writings.

William of Ockham (1288-1348) was the first to suggest that theology and natural philosophy should be independent disciplines. Ockham wanted to focus on the seen world and not be held up by metaphysics, whose centre, God, was the subject of theology. In part, Ockham was responding to Duns Scotus (1226-1308) who tended to emphasize the unity of the unseen world, termed an *univocal* understanding. Ockham believed that Duns Scotus' view emphasized unity at the expense of diversity—an *equivocal* understanding. Ockham jibed that according to Scotus' view of *Meta-*

*physics*, "at the movement of my finger the whole universe, that is heaven and earth, would be at once filled with accidents (or resulting motion)."[12]

Ockham's thought accelerated the growing distance between natural philosophy and theology, but natural philosophy eventually sought to break free from Aristotle himself. Although Aristotle never thought he had provided a final explanation for all things, he tended to be held in this regard in the medieval university. The regard for Aristotle was somewhat stifling because his understanding of mathematics (he did not believe in irrational numbers) and physics (he believed in only four elements: earth, fire, water, and air) was primitive by today's standards. Yet Aristotle still tended to be regarded as infallible.

## The Age of Enlightenment

After Ockham, important discoveries began to confirm growing doubts about Aristotle's thought. The discovery of the New World by Columbus in 1492 contradicted Aristotle's belief that the known world in his time comprised all of the land on earth. But the biggest embarrassment to Aristotelianism came in 1610 with Galileo's (1564-1642) observation of the planets through the newly-invented telescope. Galileo saw that Jupiter had moons which revolved around the heavenly body; this contradicted Aristotle's belief that all heavenly bodies revolved around the earth. Further discoveries with the telescope, especially Kepler's (1571-1630) discovery that the earth rotated around the sun, further refuted Aristotle's thought about the motion of heavenly bodies.[13]

[12] Frederick Copleston, *History of Philosophy* (London, 2003), vol 3, *Late Medieval and Renaissance Philosophy*, 70.
[13] Grant, *Foundation of Modern Science in the Middle Ages,* 167.

After some three hundred years of domination, medievals were forced to realize there were errors in Aristotle's philosophy. It was not just Aristotle who was thought to be wrong, however. The Western Church had integrated the thought of Aristotle with its theology. Theology held sway over Aristotle, but because the scriptures seemed to confirm Aristotle's ideas concerning the motion of heavenly bodies, it was simply assumed that Aristotle was right. The discoveries of Galileo and Kepler showed that natural philosophy (or science) had come of age. The Church could not claim authority in all areas of knowledge.

As natural philosophy developed in the West, the Church and ultimately the prominence of theology in the university began to decline. Martin Luther (1483-1546) sparked the Protestant Reformation in 1517 by nailing his 95 Theses to the church door in Wittenberg. This nationalized the Church, and caused it to be divided between Catholics and the various national churches (ultimately Protestant denominations). The division of the Church sparked religious tensions and wars, leading to great instability in Europe.

The Christian view of reality held sway among Europeans but through movements like the Renaissance and the discoveries of Galileo and Columbus, humans saw themselves entering a new age: The Age of Enlightenment or the Age of Reason. The spirit of the new age is seen in thinkers like Rene Descartes (1596-1650), who was weary with Aristotelianism and other past learning. For Descartes, ancient learning, was like a medieval city which had been built without any plan or order; he wanted to level the city and start again. Descartes had seen the value of this approach in his mathematical thought (which began coordinate geometry), and he believed he would have similar success in philosophy.

It is at this point that we can no longer avoid talking about *Epistemology*, the second peak in the philosophical mountain range and the assumption I will address in Chapter Five. The Age of Enlightenment did not begin from a change in how people saw reality, but from newfound confidence in *reason,* which powered the rise of science in the university. Ontology is intricately related to Epistemology, and the rise of reason began to change Western perceptions of reality.

We shall resume the discussion on Ontology as it relates to Epistemology in Chapter Five, but at this point take a break and celebrate: you have ascended the first and most difficult peak of the mountain range! There are three philosophical peaks remaining, but having climbed this one you are now in excellent shape to climb the others. We shall rejoin the story of Ontology later; but for now, Nate and I were doing some climbing of our own through the hills of Pennsylvania, listening to "Casey Jones" by *The Grateful Dead.*

# CHAPTER 4

## *The Bus goes South*

The empty winding roads near State College turned into a sea of cars as we approached New York City. It was hard to believe that we'd begun the day driving through the quiet streets of Mercer. Our small-town existence of house painting, visiting Uncle Synick, and hanging out with Nate's friends was now a fading memory. The tallest building in Mercer was three stories. In Manhattan, *all* of the buildings were higher than three stories. We were in a different world.

Nate, having the time of his life driving in the mayhem of New York City, wasn't at all fazed by our new surroundings. He loved showing off The Bus and honing his driving skills.

"This is awesome, man; I just love poking her nose out at intersections," said Nate, shifting up gears after a turn.

I was also excited by the new environs. We had been planning this trip for months and now it was a reality. We had a painting job lined up in Atlanta, and after that we had an open road. Nate was keen on driving west and heading through South America to Belize, but there was also the option of going to Florida and taking a Caribbean cruise. I was simply happy to be on the road. All had gone according to plan so far, with the exception of Nate getting constipated just before we left.

I had been to New York City once before, and it was good to be back. New York is unique, with a pulse and beat all its own. Nate and I hadn't discussed where we were going to sleep, but that question was soon answered when Nate saw a hand-painted sign advertising overnight parking for $10. Nate found a parking attendant patrolling the lot and handed him $10 for a spot—and deluxe accommodation for two in downtown New York!

By the time we had locked up The Bus it was late afternoon. Our plan was to hang out for a few hours in the city and find some food. We weren't far from Times Square so we decided to walk there and see what we could find. At that time Times Square was almost nothing but sex shops. We did manage to find some cheap fast food, and after several hours of wandering the streets, we headed back to The Bus to get some sleep.

Living in The Bus, which officially started that night, was a new experience for me. Our sleeping quarters were in the back— Nate had one side and I had the other: the back seat folded down to make a red vinyl mattress. The Bus also had a sink and plenty of storage space for our belongings.

Within half an hour, in complete darkness, I managed to change into my bedclothes, brush my teeth, and crawl into my sleeping bag. Nate, a veteran at sleeping in The Bus, was in bed long before me. The life of cheapskating was new; I would have just found a hostel, but I assumed Nate knew what he was doing.

Nate and I had no schedule or alarm clock to answer to, and we slept peacefully. The next morning, New York started buzzing again. Nate and I were sound asleep in The Bus— officially on vacation. Our plan was to sleep as late as we could to avoid rush hour traffic.

Soon after seven o'clock, however, I heard some shouting and bashing on the side of The Bus. I was deep in slumber, and Nate was the first to realize what was going on.

"Brett, we gotta get movin'," he said, rummaging through The Bus in search of his pants. "I can't believe we forgot to bring the curtains."

"What's going on?" I mumbled.

"The parking attendant must have seen us sleeping in here —I can't believe we forgot!"

The curtains were vital to our covert operation. The windows at the back of The Bus were clear, enabling a person to see in. If they got close enough they could see a bare foot or hand.

Nate had mentioned the curtains a few times when we were in Mercer, but this small detail got lost in the rush to leave.

Everything happened so fast that I was still in bed when Nate drove us out of the parking lot.

"Well, at least we're getting an early start," said Nate, who was wearing only a towel to cover himself.

Thus concluded our stay in New York City. Nate got us out of Manhattan; I lay in the back of The Bus, the engine purring beneath me. After a while I got up and rinsed my contact lenses, changed, found a breakfast bar. and climbed into the front seat. It was my first day living in The Bus, and already I was beginning to appreciate the simple life.

I tended to be somewhat cautious; Nate was my polar opposite. There is something to be said for both attitudes, and through the course of out trip we each arrived at a healthier perspective. Nate's attitude toward his constipation had become less carefree after three days, however, it was now starting to get to him.

"You know, Brett, I hadn't thought about it much but now I know what it's like in nursing homes for old folks. It's like the highlight of your day when you can sit on the can and get a good result...you're so excited you want to start boasting."

Our plan for the day was to visit Washington DC and then head as far south as we could. We had to begin our painting job in Atlanta in three days' time. Nate had intended to change out of his towel, but after several gas station stops he was still wearing it.

"I wonder how long I can keep this up?" Nate said. "It's comfortable, nobody's said anything...Yeah, I wanna see how long I can travel wearing a towel."

As we drove through New Jersey, Nate's hour of need suddenly came.

"Man, I really gotta go," he said, slightly panicked. "I knew this was gonna happen sooner or later, but rush hour…"

New Jersey was not on our itinerary but it was now…in a big way. Nate took the first highway exit he could find, looking for anywhere he could relieve himself in relative privacy. We drove into a neighborhood and saw a quiet alley. Nate slammed on the brakes and ran, yelling as he went, "Brett, keep a watch on the alley… Don't let anyone walk down here."

I kept guard as Nate disappeared down the alley. Thankfully, no one came. After about five minutes, Nate emerged a changed man.

"Man, you gotta come back here and see what I did."

"Uh…I'll just take your word for it, Nate."

"It seriously smells back there, even after I covered it up with a cement block. I feel sorry for the guy who's gotta pick that up some day."

I ventured within about twenty feet of the concrete block and decided that was my limit.

"After all that, I need to rest a little, man. Let's find a beach and chill out."

I had brought my wetsuit and body board on the trip, and I decided to do some surfing. The waves in New Jersey were nowhere near as big as those in Margaret River (in Western Australia), where I had grown up, but it was fun to be out in the ocean again. In many ways, the ocean provided a sanctuary for me when I was at university in Perth. Fortunately, UWA (University of Western Australia) was close to the beach. Before a morning lecture I could have an early morning surf and be in good sprits for the morning lecture.

After an hour of surfing the waves of New Jersey, I paddled in to shore.

"Looked like you were having fun," Nate said. He seemed to have recovered from his ordeal.

"Yeah, I had no idea you could go surfing in New Jersey."

"We should probably get back on the road again so we can get to DC in good time. It's your first visit, right?"

"Yeah, it will be," I said.

"You'll like it, man, lots of important stuff there. I always like going to DC." Nate gathered up his towel; here, he gave up his experiment—he didn't tell me why, but it may have had something to do with his alley experience.

I changed out of my wetsuit and dried myself off. University life was a distant memory, even though exams at Penn State were just a few months behind me.

By the time we got to DC, my wetsuit was well and truly dry. It was turning into quite a hot day in the nation's capital. We managed to find a place to park, but we had a ways to walk to the Lincoln Memorial. En route, we passed merchants selling drinks and trinkets. Although it was heating up, there was a sense of excitement at visiting the nation's capital in the air.

When I first saw the Lincoln Memorial reflecting pool, all I could think about was the scene in *Forest Gump*[1]. Forest is speaking at an anti-Vietnam war rally when Jenny, his long-lost friend, recognizes him and runs through the reflecting pool to embrace

---

[1] *Forest Gump*, written by Eric Roth and Winston Groom, dir. Robert Zemickis (Paramount Pictures, 1994), DVD.

him. I am sure other visitors had deeper thoughts on their minds as they saw the Washington Monument and Capitol Building rise in the distance. These monuments and buildings symbolized a lot of history. At the time, I wasn't that familiar with the American story, but this was an excellent place to begin understanding it.

After visiting the surrounding war memorials, we made our way toward the towering obelisk in the distance. At the time it was completed (1884) the Washington Monument was the tallest building in the world—such was the esteem in which the great man was held. After taking in the obelisk we made our way towards the White House, where at the time Bill and Hillary Clinton lived. There was no sign of anyone, however, when Nate and I arrived.

It was a long walk to the White House, but it was an even longer walk to the Capitol Building. The distances involved in walking between the different monuments were greater than they seemed, and combined with a rather hot day it was quite a workout, even for a relatively fit twenty-year-old. We made our way up the National Mall and took in the impressive white building ahead. Previously I had only seen these buildings in books or on TV; now they were right in front of me.

It seemed fitting that I begin my trip around the United States in DC. Throughout the trip Nate and I encountered many different people in various parts of the country. Along the way we heard all manner of accents and saw many different landscapes. But in DC all this diversity came together. The people Nate and I met had different stories, but they were all united by the story symbolized here.

"I guess we should hit the road soon," Nate said as he jostled his way through the crowd inside the Capitol Building. "Be good to clock some more miles before the day's over."

"Yeah, I don't think I'm going to see much with all these people here," I said, looking up at the ceiling.

It was a long walk back to The Bus, and we took the time to discuss our sleeping strategy. We didn't want a repeat of the morning's events, so we decided it would be best if we parked The Bus in less urban areas. Before we left Washington, Nate checked the oil and added a bottle. The Bus burned oil constantly.

Before long we were back on the freeway heading south. Although The Bus was the slowest vehicle out there, I loved the view of the open road. It almost gave the sensation that you were flying. The only thing between us and the horizon was a windscreen and a black Buddha figure atop the dashboard. Nate had put it there mostly as a cosmetic addition, but he also believed the Buddha would grant us favor on our journey.

I wasn't religious, but as the academic term had wound down at Penn State, I'd started to get interested in books on spirituality after reading *Dare To Be Yourself*[2] by Alan Cohen. I had glanced at self-help books before, but I had not read any which discussed spiritualism. Reading wisdom from Buddha, Jesus, and other spiritual characters fascinated me. I liked Cohen's notion of *daring to be yourself.* Instead of trying to fit in with everyone else, Cohen said we should simply be who we are. For me, this was a refreshing idea. I think one reason I liked Nate was that he didn't seem concerned about what people thought of him. Nate, on the whole, was content to be Nate.

In his book, Cohen tells the story of a Golden Buddha in

---

[2] Cohen, Alan. *Dare to be Yourself.* (New York: Random House, 1991)

Thailand. The people of a Thai village constructed a massive Golden Buddha sometime during the Sukkothai period (roughly between 1400 and 1550). After the Golden Buddha was completed, the political situation in the region became unstable. Fearing the Buddha might be destroyed for its gold, the villagers covered its surface with concrete to make it less appealing to potential raiders. The instability continued for many years, and eventually all the villagers who knew the secret of the Golden Buddha passed away. The new generation thought the Buddha was only concrete.

Cohen points out that many of us see ourselves as the Concrete Buddha and not the Golden Buddha. Through what we hear from others and from our culture, our estimation of ourselves diminishes. Central to Cohen's book is the idea of unearthing who we really are so we can "quit being an extra in other people's movies and become the stars of our own."

Cohen's ideas got me thinking about who I was in the world. Prior to reading his book I had pretty much accepted that I was a fortunate product of evolution; I was lucky to be alive and on top in the survival of the fittest. But this story didn't make me feel lucky or special—surely everyone else living in the world was lucky and special too. I had been striving for recognition in my various life pursuits, but I felt this pursuit was a result of my diminished idea about who I actually was. I felt I had to cover up my real self with achievements and social status points.

My dilemma was that, having achieved some measure of success in my life, I still felt unfulfilled. I was far from being a rock star or a billionaire, but I was fearful that even if I did achieve great things I would still be unfulfilled. What I saw in Cohen's book was a chance to get off this treadmill. What if the real me, at a metaphysical level, was already special and highly valued? Would a life of trying to add value to myself then be wasted effort? What if I just had to get rid of my various masks and let the real me emerge?

Cohen's ideas and the ideas of the spiritual writing he quoted opened up a new world, taking me out of my known existence and into another, in a manner similar to Bilbo leaving the Shire with Gandalf. I hadn't considered spiritual writing before, but now I was very interested. What if there really was a spirit world out there? What if characters from the past like Jesus and Buddha were onto something? Perhaps the words and thoughts of ancient spiritual masters could help me in my path through life.

As I read about these new ideas during the last few weeks of term, I felt a sense of excitement. Spiritual writings provided a newfound source of life. As The Bus wound its way through Virginia and the Carolinas, the green, lush countryside resonated with the new place I felt my life was heading. How this whole trip had come together—and the already-bizarre nature of it—made me sense it was no ordinary journey. I felt expectant in a way I had never known, like I was being led into a different mode of existence.

Evening approached, and we set up camp in someone's field. It was time to break out the canned food and enjoy deluxe cuisine.

"Well, this is great," Nate said, opening a can of baked beans. "We pay nothing to park and there's no parking attendant to wake us up!" It always amazed me how content Nate was in situations like these—you'd think he was sitting in a five-star hotel in a tropical island paradise.

Finishing up his beans, he said, "I guess we should put some camouflage on The Bus so that no one sees us."

We found some branches, and by the time we finished there was little chance we would be disturbed during the night. It was probably overkill, but a mysterious white Bus parked in a green field might have raised questions.

There were no interruptions in our sleep that night. We woke up well-rested in a forest of our own making. Taking the green branches off The Bus, we got ourselves ready. We had a hostel booked in Atlanta for the next night, the plan was to get as close as we could and sleep in The Bus for one more night. Nate got us back onto the highway, and after stopping at a gas station to refuel we were back on the road.

On the roof of The Bus, Nate had an ongoing tally of how many vehicles The Bus had passed on its many journeys. It had a top speed of 55 miles per hour, which meant we were overtaken by just about everybody. We would often see trucks and semis, sometimes towing massive trailers, steam past us uphill. There were a few occasions where we actually added to the tally, but the only one I remember was when we overtook a car in Mercer only to find it preparing to turn.

Although we didn't get any speeding tickets while driving The Bus, we accumulated a few parking tickets over the course of our adventure. In Australia I always paid my parking tickets, but Nate was less concerned; "Ah parking tickets," he'd say, "I use' em as toilet paper—if you're across state lines, man, you can use' em to wipe your ass." My hunch was that he didn't pay the tickets after he wiped himself with them.

During our journey south Nate played "Wasting Away in Margaritaville" by Jimmy Buffet repeatedly. I think Nate was hoping we would find a Margaritaville filled with some Mexican cuties on our adventure. Another song we played a lot was "Casey Jones" by The Grateful Dead. In a lot of ways we were both trying to escape the norm on this trip—looking for something more in life. I think Nate had more definite ideas about what that looked like, however.

As we entered Atlanta suburbia, we began to think about where we were going to spend the night. We were ahead of schedule, and according to Nate's travel philosophy that meant: where can we stay in Atlanta for free? It was easy to find an open field in the middle of North Carolina, but it was another to find open spaces in a major city.

Atlanta, of course, was gearing up for the '96 Olympics, and they were on the lookout for free loaders like Nate and I. We wound up sleeping in a small city park in a rich neighborhood. We decided to sleep outside The Bus because the streets were well-lit and we would be a little harder to track in the middle of a large park. The Atlanta police department, however, was up to the challenge. Neighbors must have alerted them; the sight of our '69 Volkswagen Bus looked suspicious, and the sleeping bags and pillows we took out of The Bus confirmed our intentions. As we settled in for the night, a police search party equipped with tracker dogs was dispatched. I was almost asleep when I saw flashlights in the distance.

"Nate, I think we need to leave."

"Nah, don't worry man. It'll be fine." Nate was laying happily in his sleeping bag, almost asleep.

The flashlights approached; Nate's confidence that we were going to elude a police search unit equipped with tracker dogs amazed me. I now suspect Nate was oblivious to the approaching search unit and thought I was being paranoid. While I generally liked Nate's relaxed attitude, in moments like these I felt very different.

The lights progressed towards us, and a few moments later we were surrounded by at least six police officers, completely illuminated by their search lights. Nate awoke. I remember the relaxed smile on his face.

"Good evening, gentlemen. Can we ask what you're doing here this evening?"

"Well, we're just camping out for the night. Great night isn't it?" Nate said cheerfully.

"Do you both realize it's illegal to camp out in an Atlanta city park?" said the deep voice.

"Well," Nate said, pointing at me, "he's from Australia, and that's what they do down there."

By this stage, the officers had realized their operation was overkill for dealing with two country bumpkins, and they were somewhat amused by Nate's upbeat response. They gave us a warning and we made our way back to The Bus to look for alternate accommodation. I honestly don't remember where we parked for the remainder of the night, but I remember looking forward to legitimate beds at the hostel.

The next morning, we awoke safe and sound. We didn't say much as we made our way to the hostel. Humorous as the events of the night before were, I suspect Nate was embarrassed. He saw himself as the experienced tour guide of his home country, and getting chased out of a park by a team of Atlanta police officers and tracker dogs shook him slightly. Nate was, however, reliable with the orienteering aspect of being a tour guide. Together with my map reading, we found our way to the hostel without trouble.

"Here we are, man," said Nate. "I told you the Buddha would help us get here."

Although a little precarious at times, our journey had been a success. If we had had divine assistance, then I was happy to receive it. It was mid-morning when we arrived; our beds were mattresses in a spacious but dark basement. Despite our humble lodgings, we were happy to have a legitimate bed to sleep in.

# CHAPTER 5

## *To Press or not to Press*

"Beep…beep…beep…beep…" As Desmond emerges from sleep, he hears the familiar sound of the alarm and ambles out of bed. He enters the numbers 4 – 8 –15 –16 – 23 – 42 and presses EXECUTE; the clock flutters for a few seconds, and then resets to 108 minutes. With the clock reset, Desmond turns on some music and gets on his exercise bike. After finishing his daily workout, he takes a shower, does some washing, makes a fruit smoothie and starts taking his daily medication. In a few minutes, the button will need to be pushed again.

For the last three years, Desmond has lived in an underground hatch on The Island, resetting the clock every 108 minutes. Three years before the Losties arrived, Desmond set out on an around-the-world yacht race to prove his worth to the father of Penelope, the woman he loved. Desmond's boat was caught in a storm, however, and ran aground on The Island. Kelvin, Desmond's predecessor in the hatch, rescued Desmond from the sea.

Several weeks after the crash of Oceanic 815, Locke and his fellow Lostie, Boone, are walking deep in the jungle at night. When Locke hands Boone a flashlight to navigate home, Boone drops it. They hear a clang. Alarmed at the metallic noise, the two men search the jungle floor and discover a steel door to a concrete bunker. The only way in is through a tightly-locked hatch door. Locke and Boone spend many days attempting to open it; when the other Losties eventually find out about the bunker, they end up using dynamite to blast open the door.

The blast happens while Desmond is taking his daily medication. Jack, Kate, and Locke descend into the bunker and overpower Desmond. Before he is overpowered, however, Desmond captures Locke and makes him push the button to reset the clock. In the ensuing struggle, the Losties break the computer; Desmond scrambles to fix it. In 97 minutes the button must be pushed again. Locke helps Desmond while Jack watches their efforts in disbelief. When Jack can't stand it any longer, he takes a jar of computer parts ransom and says, "Now, you're going to tell me what's going on."

"Jack, we don't have time for..." Locke replies.

"We're taking a time out."

"Please, just let me..."

"Look, you want to get to work—you're going to tell me how you got here," Jack says to Desmond.

"It was three years ago," Desmond speaks with a distinctly Scottish accent. "I was in a solo race around the world; my boat crashed into the reef, and Kelvin came."

"Kelvin?" says Locke.

"Kelvin—he comes running out of the jungle—hurry, hurry, come with me. He brings me down here. The first thing he does, because it's beeping already, is he types in the code, he pushes the button, and it stops.

'What was all that about?' I say.

"'Just saving the world,' he says."

"Saving the world?" repeats Jack.

"His words, not mine," Desmond says. "So I start pushin' the button too and we saved the world together for a while and that was lovely. Then Kelvin died and now here I am all alone…The end."

Jack reluctantly hands over the jar and Desmond continues his frantic efforts to fix the computer. Jack is not satisfied, however, and turns to Locke: "Don't tell me you believe this. This is crazy. You think that makes sense—pushing a button? You're going to take his word for it?"

"His word is all we have, Jack."

"You don't have to take my word for it," says Desmond, "Watch the film."

"What?" says Jack.

"The bookcase—top shelf, behind *Turn of the Screw*—projector's in the pantry."

As Jack and Locke set up a reel-to-reel projector, Jack says to Locke, "You understand: what he is saying is… It's insane. It's impossible."

"Why is it insane?"

"Because the last time I saw a computer that was going to save the world, it didn't look like that."

The story of the hatch illustrates a classic philosophical conundrum. Desmond enters the numbers 4 – 8 – 15 – 16 – 23 – 42 into a computer every 108 minutes, presses EXECUTE, and believes he is saving the world. The problem is that whenever he pushes EXECUTE, there is no physical evidence that his button-pushing does anything other than reset an alarm clock. Conversely, there is no evidence that his button-pushing doesn't save the world. The conundrum is: How can Jack know that this whole operation is insane and impossible? How can Locke know that the button should be pressed?

The conundrum concerning the button brings us to the next peak in the philosophical mountain range: *Epistemology*, or the possession and nature of knowledge. The ancient Greeks began formal speculations on the nature of knowledge and the word *Epistemology* is derived from the Greek word *episteme* (επιστημή), which means knowledge. However, the word *Epistemology* wasn't actually used in English until the nineteenth century.

To better understand the dispute in the hatch between Jack, Locke, and Desmond we must examine what is meant by *knowledge* and how one can *gain knowledge*. In order to do this, we must go back about two-and-a-half thousand years and stop again at the cabins of Socrates, Plato, and Aristotle, all of whom we visited in Chapter Three. Having read Chapter Three, you will be more comfortable with them, but as we are going to spend a solid seven pages with their thought, feel free to take a breather and make yourself a hot drink before we begin.

The question, *What is knowledge?* began a famous conversation more than two millennia ago. This conversation is recorded in Plato's *Theatetus,* during which Theatetus (a student of Socrates) suggests that knowledge is *perception* or information picked up by various senses. In making this suggestion, Theatetus follows the ideas of the philosopher Protagoras (490-420 BCE), who reasons that all people have an equal claim to truth because knowledge is only what is sensed.

Socrates had doubts about this line of thought. If knowledge is only what is sensed, what do we do with *memory?* What is stored in memory may have at one point been sensory information, but it is now stored information only directly accessible by the person who once sensed it. The theory of Protagoras is incomplete; it does not include knowledge from memory.

Socrates also doubts Protagoras' idea that all people have an equal claim on truth. He points out that if everyone had an equal claim on truth, it would be quite strange for people to pay and prefer certain others for *their* knowledge. When shipwreck is imminent, the people on the boat seek out the captain rather than the cook. This reliance on specialist knowledge, like that of ship captains and doctors, is hard to explain if all people have an equal claim on truth.

Sensing Socrates is right, Theatetus changes his strategy and suggests that knowledge is *true judgment* or correct understanding of the information that is sensed. Socrates says he has previously thought about this definition, but he realized that before he could deal with *true judgment* he must first deal with *false judgment*. If *incorrect* understanding of sensory information does not count as knowledge, then what is it?

Socrates attempts to explain false judgment by asking Theatetus to imagine that the soul of man is like a wax block. When a man receives sensory data, this sensory data leaves imprints upon his wax block. The man gains knowledge through recording and labeling impressions on his wax block in much the way a computer hard disk records and labels data. False judgment, according to Socrates, happens when the man *falsely* labels impressions recorded on his wax block.

To illustrate: one day I am looking through my friend Jenny's photographs, and a certain woman catches my eye. Jenny, who only met this woman briefly, says, "That's Betsy," but the woman's name is actually Sylvia. Jenny met Betsy and Sylvia, who are of similar height and have dark hair, on the same day and got them mixed up. I thus have an impression of *Sylvia* on my wax block but, following my friend Jenny's mistake, I falsely assign the name *Betsy* to this impression. It is through this kind of labeling error that Socrates attempts to account for false judgment.

Socrates then points out that the problem with Theatetus'

theory is that it does not address how one would ever realize he had made a false judgment. What if Jenny never informs me of her mistake? (Remember, this is an abstract illustration; I cannot simply ask the woman in question what her name is). Socrates finds this analogy of false judgment incomplete because there is no way to check whether the impressions on my wax block are correctly labeled. I can only assume.

Socrates' investigation shows that knowledge is more than just impressions in our brain. It includes the ways in which we *label* and *interpret* those impressions. In this way, Socrates expands on Protagoras' theory that knowledge is only what is sensed. My wax impression of Sylvia was accurate; my wrong labeling of that impression made my apparent knowledge false judgment. Socrates' point is that if I can make a false judgment in the simple process of labeling people, then of course I can go wrong in learning how to sail a ship or understanding how the human body works.

Protagoras didn't have a problem with false judgment because he believed knowledge was *only* impressions on the wax block. In this way he made knowledge, or sensory data, entirely equivalent to truth. According to Protagoras' theory of knowledge, there would be no need for doctors, lawyers and ship captains to receive any sort of training because everyone has an equal claim on truth. Socrates' view of knowledge was more complete, but it raised the problem of false judgment. If knowledge has to do with labeling objects, how can a person ever know his or her labels are correct? My friend Jenny may eventually realize her mistake and tell me she confused Sylvia and Betsy, but my potential knowledge of the intricacies of performing successful surgery may not be as easy to correct.

The problem with Socrates' wax block illustration is that there is no reliable *reference point* against which to check my labeling or judgment. There is no yearbook with which I can verify the label I have applied to my impression of Sylvia. Socrates' illustration shows how I can incorrectly label impressions, but it does not include a mechanism to check.

## Plato

The need for a reference point against which to check knowledge was seen by Socrates' student, Plato. Because the material world was temporary and always changing, Plato knew he had to look elsewhere for a permanent reference point. Plato wasn't just looking for a yearbook, but a reference point against which *all knowledge* could be checked. As a result, he developed the theory of forms mentioned in Chapter Three.

Plato's Epistemology is famously illustrated in his *Republic* by the image of a cave. People stand in a dark cave, facing the back wall. Their movement is locked; they can only face that wall. On the wall, they see moving images which they believe are real. But the images are mere projections. Behind the people is a stand with various real objects on it. A fire behind the stand projects these real objects onto the wall.

For Plato, the invisible world of forms is the reference point for knowledge. Knowledge is not the projected images, but the real objects on the stand. Visible objects in the world of substance are merely projections or shadows of the permanent world of forms. According to Plato's view of reality, only the forms count as knowledge, not individual objects in the world of substance. The world of forms (the hub and spokes of Plato's ontological wheel) comprises permanent reality and is thus the reference point for knowledge.

In Chapter Three we saw that Plato focused on the world of forms but neglected particular objects in the world of substance. From Plato's theory of knowledge we can see that his Epistemology is closely related to his Ontology—Plato's views on the nature of reality transfer through to his Epistemology. The close relationship between Plato's Epistemology and his Ontology is, in fact, not unique. A philosopher's understanding of knowledge is directly related to how he or she perceives the nature of reality.

The problem with Plato's reference point of knowledge is that it does not really solve Socrates' dilemma. The name of my romantic interest: Sylvia, does not fall within Plato's reference point of knowledge: the world of forms. For Plato, individual objects (including people) do not count as knowledge; only the human *form* is counted as knowledge. Plato did come up with a stable reference point, but the world of forms does not provide the yearbook or reference point by which I can verify my impression of Sylvia.

Plato thus had a gap problem in regard to both his Ontology and his Epistemology. Plato did not include knowledge of *particular* objects in his system. This caused a major inconsistency in his thought because he was actually using objects from the world of substance, such as the sailing of ships, to make philosophic points.

In other words, in his discussions with people Plato assumed that the seen world counted as knowledge, but in his philosophical system the seen world did not. Plato himself was uneasy with the implications of his thought, but he couldn't go back on his idea that the forms were central to the nature of reality.

## Aristotle

Aristotle was aware of the inconsistency in Plato and realized that he had to include the visible world in his philosophy. According to Aristotle, what a person senses from the visible world is called *experience*. Experience is not in itself knowledge but it offers the *starting point* for knowledge. Knowledge comes from *understanding experience*. Aristotle called the science of understanding experience *art*. For Aristotle, the visible world counts as knowledge on the condition that it is *interpreted* and *understood*. Sensations from the visible world without any interpretation did not count as knowledge because the visible world was always changing.

Aristotle believed individual objects in the world of substance were ultimately incarnations of an object's essence. The distinct essence of all objects collectively formed the unseen world of *prime matter*; this formed the reference point for Aristotle's philosophy or *Metaphysics*. The visible form and motion of each object *corresponded* to its essence. The form and motion of an object in the seen world thus helped explain the essence of that object. Whilst the seen world of *substance* was something of a lesser world for Aristotle, it was the doorway through which one could understand essence. In Aristotle's philosophical system the visible world was treated much more seriously.

By including interpretation of the visible world in his philosophy, Aristotle further expanded what counts as knowledge. But including the visible world also increased the potential for false judgment. The problem for Aristotle was that there was no guarantee that he was correctly interpreting the world of substance through his four causal questions: *formal cause, material cause, efficient cause* and *final cause*. Instead of dealing with two causes, *formal* and *material,* Aristotle dealt with the four causes of *every* object. It is one thing to determine the four causes of a table or a chair; it is another to determine the four causes of a man or a woman. The final cause of a chair is reasonably obvious: although chairs can be used in bar fights, most people will agree that they are primarily for sitting on. The final cause of a human being, however, is by no means obvious (as Chapters Nine and Eleven will discuss).

In contrast, Plato dealt only with the simpler cause questions: *formal* and *material* cause. Plato was less concerned with particular objects and more concerned with invisible forms like justice, beauty, and numbers. For Aristotle, Plato's disconnect between the seen and unseen worlds was unacceptable. Aristotle believed that the seen world of particular and changing objects was the starting point for understanding the unseen world of essence.

Aristotle included particular objects in his philosophical system, but in doing so he increased the possibility of incorrectly interpreting those objects. Aristotle was aware of the uncertainty, but he did not formally address it in his writings. Aristotle simply assumed he was more or less right because no one was able to seriously challenge him. Another fifteen hundred years would pass before some of Aristotle's interpretations of the world were challenged. Even then, critics challenged the specifics of his thought (i.e.: his belief that the sun and other planets were not actually material substances but heavenly beings), not his overall philosophical system.

While Aristotle had a stable reference point for knowledge, *Metaphysics*, he had to *interpret* the world of substance to arrive at knowledge of essence. While Plato dealt only with the *formal* and *material* cause of things, Aristotle dealt with the far more complex *efficient* and *final cause* of things. By significantly increasing the realm of knowledge, Aristotle faced an even greater reference point problem. He inadvertently created another gap, known today as *the epistemological gap*.

## The Epistemological Gap

The epistemological gap is, in simple form, the gap between *subjective* and *objective knowledge*. The epistemological gap was an important part of Danish philosopher Soren Kierkegaard's (1813-1855) thought in regard to ethics, and was further developed by Swiss theologian Karl Barth (1886-1968) in regard to theology.

It is the epistemological gap that confronts Jack, Desmond, and Locke with regard to the button. All three men sense the same data (although Desmond has been in the hatch longer than Jack or Locke and may notice more details), but they have different *interpretations* of what the button ultimately does. Their *interpretation* of what the button does is *subjective knowledge*. The *true judgment* or correct interpretation of what the button actually does is called *objective knowledge*.

As Desmond frantically repairs the computer, Jack can no longer resist challenging his interpretation: "Are you in contact with the people that made it—the film? Are you in contact with anyone?"

"Do you think I'd be here if I was?" replies Desmond.

"How is it that you didn't know about the crash? About us?"

"I push this button every 108 minutes. I don't get out much."

"So, these replacements?"

"Kelvin died waiting for his replacements."

"You don't get out; you don't see anyone. Where does your food come from? You really think this is happening?"

"Why wouldn't it be?"

"It says 'quarantine' on the inside of the hatch to keep you down here. To keep you scared. But you know what? We've been up there for over forty days and no one's gotten sick. You think that this is the only part of it that's true? Do you ever think that maybe they put you down here to push a button every hundred minutes just to see if you would? That all of this—the computer, the button—it's just a mind game? An experiment?"

"Every single day. And for all our sakes, I hope it's not real. But the film says this is an electromagnetic station. And I don't know about you, brother, but every time I walk past that concrete wall out there, my fillings hurt."

Jack and Desmond must each *interpret* what is in the hatch and hope they have made the best interpretation. Neither Jack nor Desmond has direct access to *objective knowledge* about the final cause of the button (the film by no means offers a convincing demonstration that the button saves the world), so each man makes an interpretation or arrives at *subjective knowledge*.

According to Protagoras, Theatetus' teacher, everyone has an equal claim on truth. If everyone has an equal claim on truth, the disagreement in the hatch between Jack, Desmond, and Locke is impossible. How can all three of them be right about the function of the button when Jack's interpretation diametrically opposes Desmond and Locke's? Not only does the situation in the hatch show that Protagoras is wrong in his ideas about truth, it also illustrates the *epistemological gap*.

All three men in the hatch arrive at *subjective knowledge* through interpreting what they see. But at least one of them has made a *correct* interpretation. Objective and subjective knowledge are not mutually-exclusive entities. The interpretation of Jack or the interpretation of Desmond and Locke actually lines up with truth or *objective knowledge* about the button.

For Jack, pressing the button is "insane" and "impossible"; Jack does not allow for the fact that his interpretation of the available facts might be wrong. Desmond, however, acknowledges that his interpretation or subjective knowledge could be mistaken. Jack is disturbed by the fact that two grown adults actively hold an apparently insane belief despite his best efforts to convince them otherwise. Jack cannot allow for a different interpretation because he assumes only his interpretation is the right one—that his *subjective* knowledge is actually *objective* knowledge.

Epistemological gaps are not limited to bizarre hatch situations on TV shows. While the term may sound abstract, we deal with epistemological gaps all the time, particularly in human relationships but also in the classroom. In fact, it is the crossing of epistemological gaps which makes the study of history possible. Let us take the existence of Julius Caesar, believed to have lived between 100 and 44 BCE. How is it that we can know Julius Caesar really existed?

As Caesar apparently lived and died about two thousand years ago, we can no longer obtain sensory information about the actual Julius Caesar unless we travel back in time or he manages to come back to life. As a result, we must cross an epistemological gap and make an *interpretation* regarding the data about his existence. The interpretation we make is *subjective knowledge*. The possible options are that Caesar existed two thousand years ago or he did not. Only one of these options lines up with the *objective knowledge* regarding Caesar's supposed existence (or nonexistence).

Let's say I have become a skeptic about the existence of Caesar. My interpretation of history—my *subjective knowledge*—states that Caesar did not really exist. A person who affirms Caesar's existence might counter my subjective knowledge by pointing out that many busts of Caesar have been dug up by archeologists; these busts can be claimed as evidence of his existence. This is interesting data, but the ancient Romans made many busts of gods who did not exist in the flesh and I've been told that Caesar was thought to be a god. My acknowledgement of his existence is conditional upon the fact that he actually lived in the flesh.

The person who affirms Caesar's existence might next point out that historical accounts of Caesar's life exist. In fact, many historians who lived during Caesar's time documented his life. Contemporaries such as Sallust (86–34 BCE) and Cicero (106–43 BCE) wrote about the Roman emperor. After his death, historians such as Appian (95–165 CE) and Plutarch (46–120 CE) continued to write accounts of his life.

My work is now cut out for me if I am to maintain that Caesar did not exist. I have to deal with four historical accounts which collectively affirm Caesar's existence; I must prove they are in fact flawed or false. My first line of attack is to look for unexplainable inconsistencies between the historical accounts. Proving the accounts contradict each other does not necessarily mean Caesar did not exist, but it raises serious doubts. Given that historians have poured over these accounts for two millennia without finding any unexplainable inconsistencies, it is no surprise that I am unable to find one.

My second line of attack is to suggest that the accounts are forgeries written several hundred years later by people trying to build the legend of Caesar. While it is one thing to say these accounts were forged, it is another thing to *prove* it; there already exists an entirely reasonable explanation of the data: that Caesar did exist and that the four historians gave accurate accounts of that existence. Further, I am more than seventeen-hundred years removed from the alleged forgery. Accounting for the supposed hoax would include finding out who really wrote these accounts and how they collaborated to avoid unexplainable inconsistencies.

Given that I have no evidence of an elaborate forgery, it is foolishness to hold that Caesar did not exist in the flesh. The evidence instead suggests that Caesar was a great man, and that Roman historians wrote accounts of his life. Under the weight of the evidence, I decide to abandon my theory about Caesar's non-existence and believe that the historical accounts point to his real existence. My knowledge of Caesar's existence is still *subjective,* but I believe he was real because of the serious epistemic problems that arise in believing he was not.

The options regarding Caesar are that he existed or he did not. In the hatch, pushing the button saves the world or it does not. In the dispute about Caesar's existence my opponent had an ace up his sleeve: historical accounts of Caesar. These accounts do not guarantee that my opponent is right, but they do mean that he has a much stronger hand. In the dispute about the button, however, neither Jack nor Desmond has an ace up their sleeve to account for the button saving or not saving the world.

But in the hatch, Jack seems to have the stronger hand. It just does not seem likely that pressing a button on an archaic clunker's keyboard saves the world. But the card of improbability is not enough to win the round. To say something is improbable is one thing; to say it is impossible is another. The idea of entering numbers into an archaic computer every 108 minutes to save the world seems ridiculous to Jack, but this does not ultimately prove Desmond is wrong.

In his reasoning, Jack assumes objective knowledge must be accompanied by a *reasonable account*. Desmond cannot provide Jack with a reasonable account of how pressing the button saves the world. Therefore Jack assumes Desmond is wrong. But does knowledge always have to be accompanied by a reasonable account?

By *reasonable account* I do not mean definitive proof but rather a plausible explanation of the data present. In the dispute above about Caesar, a plausible explanation of the data was that Caesar really did exist; the alleged forgery offered a less plausible explanation. My consequent belief in Caesar's existence is thus accompanied by a reasonable account. But is it true that knowledge —to count as knowledge—must always be accompanied by a reasonable account?

At one point in his discussion with Socrates, Theatetus addresses this precise issue by proposing that knowledge is *true judgment with a reasonable account*. Socrates responds to Theatetus' claim using an example from a court of law. Socrates says that a judge and jury of the court make a judgment on a particular case, but despite their good intentions their judgment is based on hearsay and bad reasoning. However, even though the court's final judgment is based on false evidence and poor reasoning, it is actually a *true judgment* that lines up with *objective knowledge*.

To illustrate, let's transpose this situation from a courtroom to a classroom. Say I am taking a calculus exam during my second year of Mechanical Engineering. My allotted time of three hours is almost up and I can't solve one of the problems. Time is ticking; the question is worth a lot of points. My equations and deductions are going nowhere. Instead of starting over, I decide to guess and make it look as though my answer follows from my equations (unfortunately, such frantic attempts to gain points are not hypothetical). Even though my equations and reasoning are bogus, my answer is actually *correct* and lines up with objective knowledge.

True judgment coming from a flawed account contradicts Theatetus' claim that knowledge must always be accompanied by a reasonable account. The mathematics faculty graders at The University of Western Australia did award me partial points for guessing the right answer. Even though my answer was *not* accompanied by a reasonable account, it lined up with objective knowledge. True knowledge does not always have to be accompanied by a reasonable account.

Of course, answers to calculus exams *should* be arrived at by a reasonable account. I would not progress far as a Mechanical Engineer relying on guesswork. Answers to mathematical problems backed by a reasonable account are more likely to be correct than guesses. Jack's assumption (that Desmond's knowledge must be accompanied by a reasonable account) works better in calculus exams than in the hatch because *different types* of knowledge are present in these situations.

Knowledge, it seems, is more like a *realm of knowledge* made up of different types. Knowledge is interpretation of what is, but different types of things exist which are either permanent (such as numbers) or temporary (such as historical events). Protagoras believed in only one type of knowledge: *sensory data*. Socrates found Protagoras' theory incomplete and expanded the definition of knowledge to include memory, knowledge of skills like sailing boats, and labeling sensory data. Plato expanded the realm of knowledge by adding the *invisible world of forms*. Aristotle further expanded knowledge by linking the world of substance with the world of essence and thereby incorporating *interpretation* of visible objects. In my examples, I have assumed knowledge also includes *mathematical and historical knowledge* as well as the function of hypothetical buttons in a TV show or other *created realities*.

Jack's assumption that knowledge must be accompanied by a reasonable explanation is not a terrible one. But this assumption does not hold true for *all kinds* of knowledge, especially when it comes to knowledge of the ultimate function of a mysterious button. Different types of knowledge are accompanied by *different* epistemological gaps. There is simply no material evidence to support or deny that pushing the button saves the world. Determining the truth of the existence of Caesar involved crossing a shorter epistemological gap because reliable historical accounts testify to his existence. Working out the answer to a calculus problem involves no epistemological gap; the answer is arrived at exclusively through deductions and logic. In this way, different epistemological gaps are associated with different kinds of knowledge.

Another type of knowledge that we haven't dealt with yet is *knowledge of people*. Who we are as people is multifaceted and complex; our individual identities are an unfolding mystery, even to us. The *mutual sharing* of knowledge of one another enables relationships. We can know people by seeing what they do and how they act, but a relationship must also include a mutual sharing of knowledge, including a person's life story, who he or she understands himself or herself to be, likes and dislikes, talents, family background, and much more. The problem we face in relationships, however, is that we have to trust the other person to share true knowledge. This is often difficult to verify.

Trusting what a person shares about him or herself, however, does not require a leap in the dark. We can do our own interpretation and evaluation of the person to check if what he or she is saying is true. Over time, we grow to trust the person because what he or she shares seems to hold together and lines up with our observations and those of other people.

The vast scope of knowledge about who a person is leads humans to rely on what is called *revelation*. Instead of checking everything that a person shares, we simply decide to trust. *Revelation* is knowledge that we accept as true on the basis of our trust in its source. Revelation is not a branch of knowledge like mathematics; rather, it is a way or *mechanism* of sharing knowledge.

Instead of being limited to my friend Jenny's photos of Sylvia, I can ask the real Sylvia to *reveal* her name. Earlier I wasn't able to do this because not all objects can tell me their name. In respect to other humans, however, I can. Instead of being limited to evaluation and interpretation, I can speak with her directly. But in asking Sylvia to reveal information, I must *trust* that what she reveals is true. Trust or belief in Sylvia is the foundation of our relationship. Faith is not just for the religious but for anyone who has friends.

In the same way that revelation enables humans to know one another, *special revelation* gives humans access to another type of knowledge: *knowledge of the gods*. Special revelation has existed since human civilization began, and knowledge of the gods comes, by and large, through various people or prophets speaking and writing for those gods. Plato affirmed multitudes of gods (although he undermined their function) as did all the cultures of his day (except for the monotheism of the Hebrews).

When dealing with the gods, God, or even no God (the atheist position) an epistemological gap always exists. In fact, apart from the discipline of *mathematics*, *every* area of knowledge contains an epistemological gap. Science relies on correctly interpreting the visible world. History relies on correctly interpreting accounts and objects from the past.

While all areas apart from mathematics have an inherent epistemological gap, *knowledge of the gods* presents us with perhaps the largest. It is important to see that this same gap exists even for atheists. To believe there is no God is as much an interpretation of reality as believing God exists (although it is more difficult to prove absence than presence).

*Knowledge of the gods* is important because it has to do with who or what is behind reality. Throughout history, philosophers have had ideas about *a foundation of being*, whether it be the *Demiurge* of Plato, *the Unmoved Mover* of Aristotle, or the *Dasein* of Heidegger. Jean-Paul Sartre (1905-1980), for example believed that the dialectic between the *in-itself* and *for-itself* was the foundation of being (more about this in Chapter Nine).

The reason all philosophers affirm a foundation of being is that *being* (however the term is defined) must originate from somewhere—whether from Immanuel Kant's (1724-1804) *divine consciousness* or Heidegger's *Dasein*. If we accept Descartes' basic tenet, *I think therefore I am,* we accept that we exist and are therefore dealing with being and its origin. Subsequently all philosophers have developed theories on the foundation of being.

While the foundation of being may seem abstract, changing ideas on this topic account for many of the different junctures in how Westerners perceive reality. The most obvious example is the conversion of the Roman Emperor Constantine, who replaced the Roman gods with the Triune God of Christianity.

If it was relatively easy to knock down pagan temples and make Christianity the official religion of the Roman Empire, it was certainly more difficult to change the foundation of being at the centre of a person's belief system. Renaming the Greek gods and worshipping them in a new form was somewhat easy, but the move from Roman paganism to Christianity represented a monumental shift. To facilitate the radical change from the typical Roman understanding of the world to a Christian understanding, new Christians in the early church were only admitted after a three-year training program (known as catechesis).

## Rise of Natural Philosophy

In our discussion of Epistemology, the transition to Christianity eventually gave rise to an important area of knowledge: *General Revelation*. General Revelation is based on a relationship between the foundation of being and how the world works. Medievals before the re-introduction of Aristotle thought it was impossible to determine how the world worked. Further, they had no idea such knowledge could be reliable.

It is at this point that we will return to the story of Ontology which I paused at the end of Chapter Three. At the time of Aquinas, the idea of the magical ontological watch still predominated in the West. Not even Aquinas himself devoted much time to figuring out how the magical watch worked. What initially drew people to the new discipline of *Natural Philosophy* was the idea of learning about God by looking at how the world worked. Even though medievals were working with Aristotle's magical watch, the vital idea that the world's movement was related to the foundation of being persisted. In short, medievals linked the character and personality of the God revealed in the scriptures with the way objects in the world moved.

While the Greek Fathers linked the *form* of things with God, medieval thinkers linked the *motion* of things with God. Over the next four hundred years, Aristotle and Aquinas' magical ontological watch became viewed as a *mechanical* ontological watch; this shift enabled the scientific revolution of the seventeenth century.

It took a long time for the medievals to modify Aristotle's ontological watch. One reason for this is the high regard in which Aristotle was held. To question the intellectual giant of the time in any area was seen as daring; for this reason, the doctrine of the four elements (fire, air, water, and earth) and the use of only rational numbers persisted in the West until the sixteenth century.

The second reason for the slow shift was the relationship between theology and natural philosophy. Initially this relationship was important because the unified and unchanging God of scripture, who desired to reveal himself to his creation, took the place of Aristotle's impersonal and removed Unmoved Mover. The relationship became problematic, however, because the *first book*—The Bible—always held sway over the *second book*—observations about the world. This tension came to a climax with the findings of Galileo, but even prior there were sharp disagreements on the occurrence of miracles and the existence of the void (or vacuum).

William of Ockham (1288-1348) first suggested that the disciplines of theology and natural philosophy should be separate. With the fall of Aristotelianism in the sixteenth century (largely due to the discovery of the New World and the work of Galileo), natural philosophy became free of theology. Natural philosophy had also been hindered by its separation from mathematics, which itself was limited by the constraints of Aristotle.

In his *Physics*, Aristotle argued that heavier objects fell at a greater speed than lighter objects. Thinkers like Galileo, however, found that they actually fell at the same speed (not including air resistance) at a constant acceleration. A hunch developed in the sixteenth century that the motion of an object was due to both its individual essence and to unseen universal forces. Rather than looking *inside* the apple to find out why it fell, Newton (1643-1727) thought something *outside* the apple caused it to fall. While Aristotle tended to theorize a one-to-one correspondence between the seen and unseen worlds, thinkers like Newton believed the universe was more complex than Aristotle realized.[1]

The work of men like Galileo and Newton culminated in the *Scientific Revolution*, the beginning of modern science. Descartes and Gottfried Leibniz (1646-1716) made important discoveries in mathematics (coordinate geometry; the development of calculus) which Newton developed and applied to the motion of the heavenly bodies. The discoveries of this age were monumental. For the first time in the history of human civilization, it became

---

[1] Aquinas also thought the connection was more complex, but he was more interested in explaining the unity of animate beings than the unity of inanimate objects.

possible to predict the course of the heavenly bodies with precision. Scientists discovered new elements and began forming the periodic table. Thinkers such as Robert Boyle (1627-1691) made important discoveries in the new and developing disciplines of chemistry and physics.

These new discoveries stirred tremendous excitement. Ideas about the world that had stood for more than two millennia had been overturned in just one century. Natural philosophy, now free of its hindrances, gave birth to the sciences. The spirit of the new age was reflected in the writings of Descartes, who aimed to level the medieval city, which represented old thought, and build a new city of truth. Western Europe saw itself emerging out of the dark ages and entering the *Age of Enlightenment*.

However, while thinkers like Descartes were overturning ideas and learning from the past, they were also borrowing ideas from the thinkers who preceeded them, sometimes without realizing it. The thought of men like Kepler, Newton, and Galileo is believed to have begun the Scientific Revolution, but in many ways they were picking fruit from a tree that had been growing for more than two thousand years.

Galileo and Newton came to different conclusions about how the world worked, but they reached these conclusions through assumptions inherited from natural philosophy—which itself came about through the integration of ideas from Aristotle and theology. Galileo, Newton, and others tweaked the magical ontological watch and overturned some past beliefs, but the scientific revolution would never have happened without vital assumptions inherited from Aristotle and theology: from Aristotle, the notion that objects' motion could be explained; from theology, the idea that the knowledge of how objects moved was related to God, who created the unseen world that caused that motion.

It is the unseen world of essence that we study in science class today. Science is not primarily concerned with objects in themselves but with how these objects *move*. Physical objects are, yes, the starting point of science but it is ultimately their *motion* that interests science. Even at a sub-atomic level the parts of an atom are always in motion. The reference point for scientific truth is not actually the material world, which is always changing, but the unseen world of essence which remains relatively constant and moves things predictably.

The orderly and predictable motion of matter is known today as *causality;* this forms the basis of modern science. The formulas and equations of modern science only work if causality is assumed. The invisible world of prime matter, or metaphysics, is the cause of this predictable motion, and it is this predictable invisible world which modern science ultimately studies.

Like all assumptions in science, sufficient basis for holding them must be shown. The basis of causality is the unseen world of prime matter. It is one thing to believe in an unseen world of prime matter, but in order for science to be a discipline, the following must be assumed: a) prime matter moves objects in an orderly and predictable way; and more importantly, b) this manner of motion holds constant. Historically, these assumptions have held true (apart from miracles), but this is no guarantee that this assumption will hold in the future. Every student and scientist does science through ongoing faith in causality.

The refinement of Aristotle's magical ontological watch into the mechanical ontological watch led to the Scientific Revolution and a new stream of knowledge: *reason*, or the ability to accurately explain the motion of objects through the assumption of causality. It was this epistemological development which led the West into the *Age of Enlightenment*.

## The Shift from Metaphysics to Ontology

The spirit of the age encouraged movement away from the superstition and mysteries of the past. But at the centre of the medieval city of thought was Aristotle. His thought enabled the scientific revolution; the reference point of his philosophy was the unseen world of prime matter or *Metaphysics*. Although Metaphysics gave birth to science, its reference point was the unseen world of prime matter.

Metaphysics presented a problem for Descartes because be could not *see* the world of prime matter. Descartes reinvented mathematics and, full of confidence in his success, turned his attention to reinventing philosophy. Descartes achieved success in mathematics by rejecting the past and proceeding logically on secure assumptions; he took this same mindset to reforming philosophy.

You may recall my earlier statement that different kinds of knowledge have different epistemological gaps. You may also recall that mathematics is the only discipline without a corresponding epistemological gap. There was thus a significant problem with what Descartes set out to do. He took a methodology that only worked in mathematics into a discipline that had always had a large epistemological gap: philosophy.

Nevertheless, Descartes proceeded to begin Modern Philosophy. The first casualty in Descartes' reformation of philosophy was *Metaphysics*. Metaphysics was the study of a world which could not be seen, so it was simply invalid according to Descartes' epistemological assumptions. Descartes' dismissal of Metaphysics, meant, however, that he had to find a new reference point with which to begin.

Finding a new reference point was vital because any discipline, to proceed, must have a *stable* reference point. Students may interpret the reference point incorrectly, but the reference point itself remains constant. Descartes also knew that he could not use the seen world of substance as a reference point because that world was always changing. The only reference point left was his own existence. Subsequently Descartes' beginning point for philosophy was, "*I think therefore I am*." Descartes doubted everything, but he could not doubt that he was doubting. He had found a new reference point with which to begin philosophy.

In making "*I think therefore I am*" his reference point, Descartes faced immediate challenges. By not using the seen or unseen world as a basis of knowledge he could no longer be certain that physical objects, even his own body, actually existed. Descartes *assumed* that physical objects did exist outside his head, but they ultimately fell outside his reference point—that same head. By proceeding in philosophy as he had done in mathematics, the only thing Descartes could be sure about was his ability to doubt. Therefore he could not be sure about the ongoing existence of physical objects.

Descartes believed he had found the reference point needed to begin modern philosophy. Subsequently he built his philosophical system upon that reference point. Indeed, the individual consciousness of each subsequent philosopher formed the new basis for philosophy. Despite its unstable and changing reference point, modern philosophy was born and Descartes was recognized as its father.

Aristotle assumed the existence of physical objects, but modern philosophers were not required to assume that what one sensed from a material object actually corresponded to an independently-existing object outside one's head. The bedrock and reference point of modern philosophy was individual consciousness, not the world of independently-existing objects. Most philosophers did assume an external world, but that world could not serve as a reference point of knowledge (except in *phenomenology*, which I will discuss in Chapter Nine). If the consciousness of the philosopher was the reference point of knowledge, then it was only the *sensations* of objects that could count as knowledge rather than objects in and of themselves.

Descartes' changing of the reference point led to the word "Ontology" supplanting Metaphysics in the seventeenth century. Ontology, or one's own interpretation of the nature of reality, replaced Metaphysics, or the unseen world of essence, as the essential reference point of philosophy.

At the beginning of Chapter Three I said that Ontology, or what it means to be, derives from our interpretation of the nature of reality. "What it means to be" is an important question, but one's own interpretation of reality is not a stable reference point. As we saw in Chapter Three, people have had varying interpretations on the nature of reality throughout history. Ontology is thus an insufficient reference point for understanding reality because it is itself already an interpretation.

## Philosophy after Descartes

After Descartes, the discipline of philosophy went into defensive mode. The first problem philosophy had to confront was the doctrine of universals, essentially Plato's world of forms, which was central to the thought of Augustine. The doctrine of universals had been a challenge for Thomas Aquinas. The modern philosophers were even more challenged because they could no longer use Metaphysics or the world of unseen prime matter to explain the world of forms.

One of the many philosophers to tackle the problem of universals was English philosopher John Locke (1632-1704). The problem facing Locke was explaining universals, such as shape and color, which seemed to repeat themselves in different objects. There had to be an ideal circle or ideal color red somewhere. Locke took up the challenge of finding them.

Locke could no longer use Augustine's *doctrine of the universals,* so he found his solution by locating the forms in the human brain. According to Locke, each object had primary and secondary qualities. The primary qualities were the universals, such as shape, color, and hotness; the secondary qualities were the particularities of each object, such as the words "Blue Parrot" on a cup or the cup's unique shape. Locke believed that the primary qualities of the cup dwelt in the human brain and the particular qualities of the cup dwelt with the object.

Locke's solution to the problem of universals contained serious flaws. First, he attempted to neatly divide universals and particulars, a problem Plato had been unable to resolve more than two thousand years prior. The words "Blue Parrot" on the cup may seem particular, but what if thousands of cups with "Blue Parrot" on them exist? Second, there was the somewhat-humorous dilemma of what happened to the cup when no one was looking if its primary qualities were located in the human brain.

While Locke was responding to the historic doctrine of universals, a more serious problem for modern philosophy loomed on the horizon: *causality*. Newton's discovery of gravitation, which accurately predicted the path of the planets, changed the way Westerners thought about the world and put *causality* in the limelight. *Causality* posed a problem for modern philosophy because it was a product of Metaphysics, the unseen world of prime matter from which modern philosophy was running away.

Scottish philosopher David Hume (1711-1776) explained causality as being able to predict events based on personal experience. But, as Immanuel Kant realized, predicting events based on past experience is not a sufficient basis for causality. Predicting events is a *result* of causality, not an account. Kant realized that modern philosophy could not continue if it was unable to explain causality and he therefore took up the challenge.

I will return to Immanuel Kant's solution to the problem of

causality in Chapter Seven. In the meantime Nate and I were quite happy to assume causality as we threw ourselves into our beds in the hostel in Atlanta after our first day painting.

# CHAPTER 6

## *Pipes and Prophets*

The house Nate and I were painting was about a ten-minute drive from the hostel. Large and white, it reminded me of scenes from *Gone With the Wind* (1939). We were working for a soft-spoken guy named Alfred who was African-American, laid back, and in his mid-forties. Alfred, who was working with his son Sidney on this enormous project, was happy Nate and I were there to lend support. As it turned out, Alfred was the perfect boss.

Before this job, Nate and I had only painted exterior walls. Now Alfred had us working on refinishing windows, which involved scraping away the glaze that seals the glass in place on the window frame. Our job was to remove the glaze, make up new glaze, put it on the window, and paint over it. With some training and experience, this job isn't difficult, but this *was* the training for Nate and I—our trial run was this house in Atlanta. Needless to say, our work had mixed results. Alfred quickly realized how incompetent we were and started giving us tips.

"You gotta paint the raw wood," he would say in his deep drawl, gesturing with his paintbrush over the wooden window frame. Upon reflection, Alfred was very gracious to Nate and me as we bumbled our way through the job. After a few days, we realized we were in over our heads. Finishing up our second day, we piled into The Bus to head back to the hostel.

"I think I only did two windows today," Nate said, steering The Bus out of the driveway onto the main road.

"Yeah, me too, and that was after Sidney spent an hour helping me out."

"This job is nothing like painting my Dad's house. I thought it would be so much easier," Nate lamented.

"What do you think we should do?" I asked, scratching white paint off my hands.

"Well, as long as Alfred is willing to pay us, I guess we just keep on going. Maybe we'll get better."

Nate and I did improve, but being competent at reglazing windows still required more training and practice than we were getting. It was a frustrating job, even for Sidney, and we were not sure how long we could keep it up or how long Alfred would put up with us. He had a business to run and he couldn't have Nate and me making mistakes all the time.

Although painting wasn't going so well, Nate and I enjoyed staying at the hostel, which was quite full. We saw a lot of friendly, interesting people coming and going. Although our sleeping space was in the basement and a little dark, it was relatively quiet—a good space to sit and rest after a day of painting.

In the course of our comings and goings at the hostel, Nate and I met Tony. Tony was in his forties, but he had the spirit of a person in his twenties. He was muscular, with a dark tan and a slightly-balding head—an attractive middle-aged man. Tony usually wore trendy clothes and sometimes carried a gnarled stick. He was outgoing, and he fit right into the urban hostel subculture. Whenever a group of young people gathered, Tony was there. Sometimes when it got dark a group of us would go for a walk, and Tony would capture everyone's attention with a story about his spiritual pilgrimage.

Once he told us about the stick he carried, which we learned had spiritual significance for him. He had asked God for some kind of sign during a difficult time in his life; very soon after, he came across an interesting stick that looked like a magician's staff. He took this to be the sign he'd prayed for; consequently, the stick became part of his persona. Combined with Tony's tie-dyed shirt, the staff made him resemble a modern-day prophet.

Tony lived in a rented house close to our lodgings; he loved hanging out at the hostel and meeting young people from all over the world. He had built a relationship with the hostel's owners and would regularly hang out there. It is unusual to meet older people in urban hostels, and even more unusual for young people to be captured and interested by them, but Tony had a unique ability to draw attention in a way that seemed completely natural.

Tony fascinated me. He was the antithesis of my image of a successful forty-year-old, yet he was someone I wanted to emulate. Tony was a free spirit and passionate about life—there was no way he was going to let the world stamp him into a mould. Before meeting Tony, I had encountered many men in their forties who were more or less cogs in the machine of a corporation. Much can be said for living a secure life, but I often felt these men were settling for less than they were capable of achieving. I didn't know where I wanted to end up, but I knew I didn't want to opt for a secure yet unfulfilling job and watch a better life pass me by.

Even though Nate and I were having a tough time painting the house, all our concerns seemed to vaporize when we returned to the hostel. Sometimes there would be new arrivals; at other times, a bunch of people we knew would be sitting around having a drink. After Nate and I had changed and showered, we entered a new world of visitors and engaging conversations.

Nate's outgoing personality, combined with the two of us coming and going from the hostel in clothes covered with white paint spots, made us an interesting pair. It was remarkable how different Nate and I were in social situations. In the space of a few days Nate had befriended just about everyone at the hostel; I was in contrast, still coming to terms with complete strangers suddenly knowing me because of Nate. Nate was a natural at meeting people from all walks of life. In my introversion, I tried to come to terms with the extra attention.

Nate found the hostel environs a refreshing change from the predictability of Mercer and State College. He was fascinated with people, but he felt tied down in the college dorm scene. On our floor in Beaver Hall, Nate was known as "Crazy Nate" because he was so different. Tony was a keen observer of people; I'm sure he was perplexed at how Nate and I had ended up traveling together.

The answer was simple: Nate and I were different, but we were on a similar path. We were both finding ourselves and wondering if anything else was out there; we were in the process of maturing. In a lot of ways, we were still boys working to become men. I think Tony knew that stage in life and sensed that, as someone who had walked similar paths, he could help us

As a young boy I had a good relationship with my dad. Due to my parents' divorce when I was twelve, however, Dad was absent during my teens. He lived about a three-hour drive away and over time our relationship became increasingly distant. My dad affirmed me as a boy but I lacked a father figure during my adolescence: the divorce splintered my family, and no one was able to fill the role of father figure. As I progressed through my teenage years, I never took stock of this void in my life—I just accepted it and moved on.

I didn't know it at the time, but I needed a father figure I respected and got along with. As it turned out, Tony was that figure for both Nate and I, supplementing the weaknesses of our own fathers. In our interactions, I felt that Tony was more often that not amused by Nate and somewhat intrigued by me. At that point in my life I don't think even I had a good read on who I was, but Tony had an uncanny ability to look beneath the surface and see people for who they really were.

After about a week at the hostel, Tony said, "Why don't you guys stay over at my place while you're doing this paint job? It's closer and you guys won't have to pay any rent."

I don't know what precipitated this invitation; I suspect Tony saw that we needed something a bit more permanent while we were in Atlanta, and I think he liked hanging out with us. Nate and I were content to stay at the hostel, but Tony had become our relational anchor. The move to his place seemed like a natural progression.

Not paying rent was also a big attraction for Nate. I don't know what went through his mind when Tony invited us to live in his house, but I can imagine a little computer in Nate's brain going, "FREE ACCOMMODATION! FREE ACCOMMODATION! WE PAY MONEY HERE at the hostel, BUT AT TONY'S WE WON'T," followed by the automatic response, "TAKE IT, TAKE IT." And so we did.

Tony lived in a rented house with a definite hippie vibe. It was rundown but cozy, the kind of place you would expect someone like Tony to live. Every room was painted a different color (the kitchen was purple) and a certain disorder made you feel comfortable. An overgrown garden made the house somewhat secluded; while we were in a large city, it often felt like we were away from it all.

Frequently, after a long day on the job we drove home to

see an extra car or two parked outside Tony's. While Nate and I were always the youngest, we were always welcomed into the conversation and cold beer sharing. A typical night consisted of people coming and going, stories, laughter, and lots of pipe smoke.

One day after we had finished work, I was sitting in the kitchen with a few guests when Tony started playing his accordion. The bathroom was directly adjacent to the kitchen, which meant that you walked straight into the kitchen after exiting the bathroom. Nate was taking a shower when the accordion show began and he walked straight into the commotion. Standing wrapped in his towel, he looked at me in comic bewilderment.

"Ha, I take a shower and now he's playing for everyone." Nate stood for a moment, taking in the music and the bizarre unpredictability of Tony's house. Nate had met a lot of characters in his lifetime, but Tony was unique.

My ordered life at Penn State felt like a distant memory as I sat amongst this hippie crowd in Atlanta, listening to Tony's music. Nate eventually changed and sat down to listen. At one point he fell asleep. I still remember the contented look on his face.

Tony had a girlfriend who would come over from time to time. I don't recall her name but I remember she was blonde and attractive, somewhere in her twenties. I didn't know the specifics of her relationship with Tony but the door was always closed when she slept over, and he would sometimes put a noisy fan outside of our room as Nate and I were getting to sleep.

Sometimes, when there were a lot of people at the house, the conversations would drift and turn. At other times it would just be Tony, Nate and I; Tony would start telling stories from his past while Nate and I lay on the floor, relaxed and content.

"Here's a story I wrote about some briar bushes," Tony would say. All his stories seemed to relate back to his spiritual path: one was about a radical conversion he had had while growing up. He came forward at a religious meeting at his high school and knelt in front, weeping before his school friends.

I had a lot of respect for Tony. He lived his life with conviction and was prepared to stand alone. His pipe smoking and loose lifestyle sometimes contradicted the depth of character I saw in him. Up until this point, I had pretty much been a boat tossed around on the ocean; I drifted with the current of trying to please people. After getting to know Tony, I knew I wanted what he had. I wanted to live with conviction, to be someone who stood for something.

Tony was secure in his masculinity, and during the time Nate and I stayed with him, I realized I was a long way from security in being a man. Tony had a confidence and maturity I hadn't seen modeled before. He wasn't Superman, but there was a strength about him—and a weakness—which he wasn't afraid to show.

Tony was in the antique business with an Australian guy named John. I don't know how they became business partners, but I guess John had the capital and Tony had the salesmanship. In Atlanta, there was lot of money to be made in antiques if you knew what you were doing.

One of the ways Tony sold antiques was through the local flea market, which drew many antique hunters willing to pay a lot for seemingly worthless items. Tony had a fascinating assortment of objects—a rusted old knife that looked like it had been recovered from a shipwreck, an antique sewing machine, various china ornaments.

Nate and I had no clue about the antique business, but we were willing to tag along and have fun. Early in the morning, we loaded up Tony's truck and The Bus with items, tied down the load, and ventured to the flea market. On one occasion Nate was tying the load using an intricate-looking knot. It seemed solid to me, but Tony wasn't so sure.

"Think that's going to hold, Nate?"

"Yeah, it's a highwayman's hitch."

"Yeah," said Tony, "think it's gonna hold if I pull on it?"

"Go ahead—it's a good knot."

"Well, watch…you ready?" He grabbed the end of the rope.

"Okay...sure," Nate said, a little less confident now.

With a good hard tug from Tony, the knot came undone. Nate stood back despondently, his knot-tying ability having suffered a somewhat public humiliation. Like me, Nate was growing in manhood. At times like this he was forced to do a reality check. Tony showed Nate how the knot was supposed to be tied, and after all was secure, Nate and I got into The Bus and followed Tony and John to the flea market.

Atlanta's flea market was about a hundred times bigger than any market I had seen before. Every time we went it was a glorious sunny day; people seemed glad to be there. The area teemed with shoppers and vendors, all eager to find or sell hidden treasure. Tony led the way, driving his blue Toyota truck through the crowd like Moses leading the Israelites through the Red Sea.

Somehow he'd find a spot. A few times an argument ensued with a nearby seller, but Tony eventually sorted it out.

For Nate and I, being with Tony offered a certain security. It didn't matter what situation came up. If Tony was there, it got sorted out. During the trip, Nate and I had to sort out some situations by ourselves, but we weren't afraid of anything when Tony was around.

What I loved most about the flea market was the variety of people: Mexicans, Asians, Europeans, and southerners all in the same place. The range of items for sale was remarkable: engine blocks, pocket knives, flower pots, antique dolls, t-shirts…there was no telling what you might find. While we were unpacking, swarms of people descended on us, searching out the hidden treasure that could make them a fortune. The variety of people who browsed our stall was a constant wonder. We saw everyone from wealthy antique collectors to little children with a dollar to spend.

Almost everyone who came by would at some stage notice the rusted pirate knife. No one knew how much it was worth, but everyone found it intriguing. Who knew what path this knife had taken through the years? All the items in our stall hinted at interesting stories: What hands had they passed through over the generations? Whose lives had they touched? Where would they go from here? Our little stall in the middle of the flea market in Atlanta symbolized so much to me; whatever path these objects had taken, their stories were temporarily joined with mine.

Sometimes Tony would wander off to look at other stalls, giving Nate and I instructions about how much to sell things for and how to sell particular items. I sold a lot of small items, but I was most proud of selling an old sewing machine. It was heavy and black, an old-style design—it looked very different from my mom's modern sewing machine. It had gone with us to numerous flea markets and we'd had numerous offers, but Tony always held firm on the $100 price. A buyer took an interest in it when Tony was not there.

"What can you tell me about that sewing machine?"

"Well, it's an antique; if it's restored, it will be worth a lot—we've been asking $200 for it," I said.

"How about I give you $50?"

"I'm sorry, but we just can't go below $100—you know, it's an antique... we just can't."

Here I expected the guy to walk away, but amazingly, he bought the sewing machine for $100 instead. I was elated. Through teaching and trusting me, Tony had enabled me to become a confident seller of antiques. If I could sell an apparently-worthless sewing machine for $100, the sky was the limit!

At the end of the day, we totaled up our earnings. Tony often gave us a generous share of the takings, even though none of the items we sold belonged to us. By this stage in our Atlanta stay, Nate and I had "finished" our painting job; we received $200 each from Alfred. It wasn't much, but neither was the quality of our labor. In the course of a few days helping Tony at the flea market, however, Nate and I earned more than in two weeks of painting. We packed all the remaining items into The Bus and navigated our way back through a sea of contented people, feeling good. We'd been part of the fun and madness of the Atlanta flea market.

One day we all went to The Further Festival, which featured some members from The Grateful Dead. The crowd resembled a kaleidoscope of purples, blues, and yellows. There were so many other busses in the lot that it was like a little family reunion for The Bus— and for the pot smokers of Atlanta.

"You guys see that line over there?" Tony said, leading us through the crowd.

"Yeah, what's it for?" asked Nate.

"It's for laughing gas, but the lines come and go—the police keep cracking down on it."

"Is there a way we can get some?" Nate asked.

"Well, if you see a line in time, yeah, but it's gonna cost you."

Nate's interest seemed to wane, but he remained curious about the mysterious lines.

Tony seemed to know a lot of people, and for about an hour, we toured the lot and befriended some of the "Dead Heads" hanging out in their vans. Nate and I were a little out of place at this gathering of people from the sixties and seventies, but we felt included nonetheless. Tony disappeared a few times during the concert, probably to get reacquainted with some old friends and find some new contacts of the feminine persuasion. For the most part, Nate and I sat on the grass and took it all in.

What fascinated us about Tony was that he was a father figure—yet he was simultaneously just like us. An unlikely prophet, he smoked, liked his women, and loved to party. But there was something about Tony that made you stop and reevaluate your life. He lived beyond the cares and worries of the world; he was a free spirit whose life seemed to go against the flow.

*Pipes and Prophets*

Once when we were sitting around the table at Tony's, clouds of smoke in the air, he pulled out his Bible and turned to the book of Genesis. All attention focussed on him. The fact that *any* book was being read in this context was unusual, but the Bible in particular demanded an explanation.

"Do you actually read that, Tony?" one of his friends asked.

"Sure," he said, thumbing through the pages.

"So you believe all that stuff…you know, Adam and Eve and all that."

"Absolutely. I believe this book is the very word of God."

"How can you believe that, Tony?"

These questions didn't faze Tony. He began reading aloud and sharing how this book had impacted him. There was no doubt that it had. For many people in the group the Bible represented legalism and rules. It was somewhat humorous that Tony of all people would hold it in the esteem that he did. Despite the irony, everybody could tell Tony meant what he said.

I had a deep respect for Tony, and his endorsement of this ancient book began a paradigm shift in my life. Previously, I had been open to basically anything with the exclusion of the Bible, which I considered an irrelevant book of mythology. I by no means rushed out the next day and bought myself a copy, but that day a subconscious shift in how I viewed the Bible took place.

Growing up, I had developed a view of the Bible similar to Jack's response to the idea that pushing the button could save the world. There was simply no way its contents could be true. Ideas of going to heaven and getting saved did not compute. I was not just ambivalent to the Christian story; I was somehow offended by it, so much so that I refused to attend a religious studies class during primary school. To believe that the Bible had anything true or important to say was an impossible epistemological gap for me to cross.

But somehow that gap became shorter when I witnessed Tony's respect for this ancient book. On July 4$^{th}$, we took a trip to Tennessee. Tony needed to put his truck in storage; he and John were about to take their antique show on the road, and Tony was moving out of the hippie shack. As we drove towards Nashville, firecrackers popped continuously and blue, red, and white flags flew in every driveway. In all my life I had never seen this kind of patriotism.

After Tony stored his truck, we drove back to Atlanta in John's truck. Tony and John were in the cab and Nate and I were in the back taking in the stars and fireworks. As the truck sped through the night, the wind blowing through our hair, I began to reflect. A few months earlier my head was buried in formulas and equations, I planned to spend my summer working in a pipe factory. Now I was riding on the back of a truck somewhere between Nashville and Atlanta in the midst of a trip around the USA.

Doing this trip with Nate in the first place was bizarre; our experience in Atlanta was something else. Fourteen years later I still stand back in wonder at how everything happened the way that it did. Our time with Tony was such an "out there" experience. It seemed like we spent a year at his house— actually, it may have only been a month. There were many highlights, including an attempt to see a Steady-Rollin Bob Margolin concert, afternoons swimming in a nearby lake, and a day at the Atlanta Six Flags amusement park.

My most vivid memories, however, are of sitting around the kitchen table pipe smoking and listening to Tony's stories late into the night. We hardly remembered that the city of Atlanta was preparing for the Olympics; we were in a world of our own. The days we stayed with Tony seemed to roll on and on, as if we could live there for an eternity. I think a part of me still longs to go back and relive the experience.

Nate and I decided to head west to California. Tony was happy for us to stay at the house, but the lease was about to expire and the landlord wouldn't be pleased with the conditions, so it was best we got going.

The day of Tony and John's departure marked the closing of a chapter in our journey. Nate and I were sad, but excited about taking The Bus on the road again. Tony gave us some last-minute instructions regarding the house and we said our farewells—I think all of us realized this was the end of something special to which we could not return. Our time together had been sacred.

Soon after Tony and John departed, Nate and I got back on the road. We decided to camp for a few days in a forest to get our bearings and transition to our existence on the road. We had been living in a different world and needed time to adjust. The middle of a forest wasn't the perfect place, but it was free. Before we began the journey west, Nate resolved to get The Bus serviced. We checked in at a somewhat dodgy looking garage and found the highway west.

The hum of The Bus engine was back in our lives as we rolled through the outskirts of Atlanta. The urban metropolis gave way to trees and open highway. We had not ventured far when I noticed The Bus was not going as fast as normal; I sensed Nate's anxiety. As The Bus continued to slow I knew we were in trouble.

"What's wrong, Nate?"

"Um…I don't know, man. I have my foot on the gas; it's not working."

"We're going to have to pull over, Nate; something's definitely wrong. Do we have enough gas?"

"Yeah, everything looks fine. Don't know what the deal is," Nate said, looking intently at the dashboard.

The engine shut down completely as we pulled over to the side of the highway. We sat in silence, cars flying by. Nate tried starting The Bus. Nothing.

We needed help: "Well, man, looks like we're walking now," said Nate. "I saw a gas station not long ago. Let's head back there."

We made it to the gas station and they summoned a tow truck. We walked back to The Bus and waited. Nate had driven The Bus for a long time. This was a tough moment. Both of us were thinking that our adventure might end on the side of a highway outside Atlanta. As we waited, Nate found a 1000-piece jigsaw in The Bus and started working on it. I tried not to laugh. The jigsaw was only partially complete when the tow truck arrived to tow away The Bus—and our aspirations for the trip.

We returned to the gas station, and their mechanic began examining The Bus. He was a burly man of few words, but he looked like he knew what he was doing. After a brief inspection he gave us the news: "The engine is locked up," he said matter-offactly. "The only way to fix it is to drop a new engine in."

Our worst fears confirmed: The Bus was dead and we were stranded at a gas station in the middle of nowhere. Fixing The Bus would cost a few thousand dollars; even worse, it would take at least three weeks. We told the mechanic our situation. His initial response was not encouraging. He took Nate inside to talk about options.

I waited, staring at The Bus, facing the grim prospect of heading home early. I had had a lot of fun already, but I wanted desperately to head west.

After a while Nate emerged from the office with a slight smile on his face.

"Brett, we may have a solution."

"Yeah?" I said, skeptical.

"There's a car they want us to take a look at."

"Where?"

"It's on this guy's farm somewhere."

"What kind of car?"

"Um…they didn't say," Nate said. "They said it's a little rough but it has a good engine. They use it on the farm."

"So what is it—a tractor?"

"Like I said, they didn't say. At this stage, man, it's our only option."

Having no idea what to expect and nothing to lose, we decided to take a look at the mystery vehicle. As we headed towards the farm, paved roads became narrow dirt tracks. In the back of my mind, I wished Tony was still with us. Now was when we needed him most.

# CHAPTER 7

## *Trouble in Paradise*

At the time of the crash of Oceanic 815, Hurley was worth $156 million dollars—he'd used the numbers 4 - 8 - 15 - 16 - 23 - 42 to win the lottery. But along with his newfound wealth came a curse for using the numbers to win. After a string of bad luck, including a meteorite striking his newly-acquired Mr. Clucks fast food store, Hurly follows a lead to Kalgoorlie, Australia to end the curse.

Unsuccessful in his quest, Hurley heads back to the States. The evening before boarding Oceanic 815, Hurley stayed in an upmarket hotel in Sydney overlooking the Sydney Opera House. On his first night on The Island, he finds shelter under a piece of wreckage on the beach. The change is symbolic of Hurley's sudden drop in financial clout.

Sleeping on the same beach as Hurley is another Lostie named Sawyer. Sawyer's real name is James; the real Sawyer was a con man that James was hunting in an attempt to avenge his mother and father's deaths. By devoting his life to the pursuit, James became the man he hunted. In the real world, Sawyer's net worth was minuscule compared to Hurley's. Within a few days of the crash, however, Sawyer scavenges enough items to surpass Hurley in financial clout. On The Island Sawyer is the rich man and Hurley the poor man.

Hurley, Sawyer, and the other Losties enter a new economic reality when they crash on The Island. Real estate, investment funds, and credit cards are no use. Rich girl Shannon is forced to bargain with Sawyer for sunscreen and flirt with Charlie to get a fish—the ocean won't take her gold card. In the world they came from, the Losties took food, shelter, and water for granted; on The Island, the ability to acquire these basic necessities is a matter of life or death.

A few days after the crash, Jack searches the cabin of the plane for medicine to help a wounded survivor. He runs into Sawyer.

"What's in the bag?" Jack inquires.

"Booze, smokes, couple of Playboys. What's in yours?"

"Medicine."

"Well, that about sums it up, don't it?"

"Do you do this back home, too—steal from the dead?"

"Brother, you've got to wake up and smell the bull crap here; rescue ain't comin'. You're just wasting your time. You're trying to save a guy who last time I checked had a piece of metal the size of my head sticking out of his bread basket. Let me ask you something: how many of those pills are you going to use to fix him up?"

"As many as it takes," Jack says.

"Yeah? How many you got? You're just not looking at the big picture, Doc. You're still back in civilization."

"Yeah? And where are you?"

"Me? I'm in the wild," says Sawyer and walks away.

In many regards the Losties *are* in the wild. Due to the political and legal vacuum in which they find themselves, they experience a reversal of economic fortunes. As far as they know, they now live in a place with no elected government, no private land, no currency, and no agreed-upon legal code. The various legal and political structures to which they are accustomed are now non-existent. The ethical understandings the Losties brought with them to The Island now have to be revised.

As the story of *Lost* develops, it becomes apparent that The Losties are not alone on The Island. Far from being in a political vacuum, they are immersed in a battle between different groups for supremacy. One of these groups, The Others, live in houses with electricity and running water. A collection of individuals who have been gradually drawn to The Island, the first known Other to arrive was Richard Alpert, who came on board the slave ship *The Black Rock* in 1867.

The Others predate another community known as the Dharma Initiative. The Dharma Initiative, created in 1970, was the brainchild of Gerald and Karen DeGroot—two doctoral candidates at the University of Michigan. The Dharma Initiative, inspired by visionaries like B.F. Skinner, set out to create a large-scale communal research compound where scientists and free thinkers from around the globe could pursue research in meteorology, psychology, parapsychology, zoology, electromagnetism, and utopian social science. With the financial backing of Danish industrialist and munitions magnate Alvar Hanso, the Dharma Initiative constructed a vast network of laboratories, tunnels, and communication stations on The Island, including the hatch.

Dharma coexisted with The Others for about thirty years; The Others inhabited the jungle while Dharma members lived in houses. However, Dharma and The Others both laid claim to The Island. The groups came to an agreement to avoid contact and Dharma constructed a protective fence around their residences as an extra security measure. They maintained an uneasy truce until several years before the Losties' 2004 crash, when The Others infiltrated Dharma with the help of Ben Linus, son of a Dharma member. The Others killed off Dharma in one foul swoop, took over their facilities, and inhabited the houses Dharma had built.

The Others elected Ben leader and lived in relative peace until, several years later, in the midst of a book study on Stephen King's *Carrie,* they heard a loud noise outside. Abandoning their study, they ran out to watch Oceanic 815 breaking apart and plummeting to Earth. After the crash, Ben asks Ethan and Goodwyn to find the front and tail sections of the wreckage and infiltrate any groups of survivors.

The Others have a problem. None of the women who become pregnant on The Island are able to carry a baby to term; something about The Island causes pregnant women and their babies to die before childbirth. The Others expend great time and resources on this problem, but until they find a solution they need to either bring in fresh recruits or kidnap children who appear on The Island.

Ethan finds the plane wreckage and successfully infiltrates the Losties; he bides his time, posing as a Canadian survivor. Among the Losties, he discovers a pregnant woman named Claire. Claire, impregnated off The Island, could be a valuable subject for the Others' research. Following orders from Ben, Ethan waits, but when Hurley finds the flight manifest and starts taking a census, Ethan realizes he will be discovered and kidnaps Claire.

The kidnapping of Claire precipitates bad relations between The Losties and The Others. The Losties eventually get Claire back, but the Others kidnap Walt, a young boy who is on The Island with his father, Michael. Using Walt as leverage, the Others turn Michael against the Losties and recruit him to help kidnap Jack, Kate, and Sawyer. At the end of Season Two of *Lost*, when Michael recovers Walt, he takes stock of what he had done to his friends and asks Ben: "Who are you people?"

Ben replies, "We're the good guys, Michael."

Ben's answer raises a question that has challenged philosophers for more than two millennia: What does it mean to be *good*?

In *Lost*, especially at first, the innocent and unsuspecting Losties are the good guys and The Others the bad guys. As the story develops, however, clear-cut distinctions between *good* and *bad* blur. Exactly what does it mean to be good? Who gets to decide? These questions bring us to the third peak of our imagined philosophic mountain range: *Ethics*.

While Ontology and Epistemology are somewhat abstract, hidden assumptions, Ethics is tangible and visible. In our action and inaction, the lives of our minds become visible. The word "ethics" comes from the Greek word εθος (*ethos*) which has to do with character and habit. Ethos is the root of ἠθικός (*ethikos*), which means *moral* or *showing moral character*. For the Greeks, both ancient and modern, *ethikos* involves understanding the inner soul and its corresponding actions. The use of the word *Ethics* to describe human action originates from classical Greek philosophy's belief that human action derives from the human soul.

In Aristotle's time, the study of Ethics had to do with understanding the inner being and its motivations. Today, Ethics has to do with the formulation of rules or laws, and being described as a *good* person often means not having broken any laws. In contrast, Aristotle linked the *good* with living a happy and contented life. The good in modern ethics is a *state* of not having broken any laws, while in Aristotle's thought, the good describes the *path* of the contented person.

Aristotle's *Politics*, written as a continuation of his *Nicomachean Ethics*, is not primarily concerned with determining the best law code. Rather, it examines how to set up a city so as to enable a group of people to become a contented community. Aristotle was not against law codes, but he knew that constructing the ideal law code was not enough in itself to ensure a city's success. While modern Ethics focuses on developing law codes, Greek Ethics dealt with understanding human action so as to enable the city's overall success. These are not unrelated ideas, but there are important differences between them.

Because Ethics is the most visible of assumptions, it has attracted philosophical attention throughout the ages. Different schools of ethical thought have arisen, especially after the English Civil War (1641-1651) and during the European Enlightenment. Prior to the Age of Enlightenment, the church influenced thought on the good through what is known as the "divine law." The church and the aristocracy were intricately connected, however, and administration of the law by the aristocracy was influenced by the church's ethical views.

During the sixteenth and seventeenth centuries, the power of the European church and aristocracy was progressively broken (usually though revolution and violence), and democratic constitutions began to replace divine law. A new way of determining the good was needed. The church based the good on interpretation of scripture; ethical thinkers of the time had to find other *reference points*. These different reference points form the different schools of ethical thought.

Aristotelian Ethics, which predates the church, is called *Ontological* Ethics because Aristotle believed the reference point lay within each human. Aristotle believed all human action tended toward some good; therefore, the reference point for ethics was fine upstanding humans like himself and ultimately the successful and contented Greek city. An example of a contemporary Ontological Ethics philosopher is Alasdair Macintyre (1929- ).

Immanuel Kant (1724-1804) believed that the reference point for the good was reason. For Kant, the reference point for Ethics had to be separate from human motivations and desires; his ethical system is thus called *Deontological* Ethics. An example of a contemporary Deontological philosopher is John Rawls (1921-2002).

Two other closely-related schools of Ethics are *Utilitarian* and *Realist* Ethics. *Realist* Ethics bases itself on preserving power by doing "whatever works". Whatever works is something of a chimera, however; this reference point changes depending on *who* the action works for and in what time frame. Robbing a bank today may pay off in the short term but not the long.

Niccolò Machiavelli (1469-1527), an Italian philosopher, is considered one of the first realists. His principles, including "It is better to be feared than loved," are drawn from his book, *The Prince*. Realist ethics did not start with Machiavelli, of course (history is full of aristocrats who did whatever it took to preserve their power), but Machiavelli was the first to formalize a code of Realist Ethics. Another notable Realist is Thomas Hobbes (1588-1679), famous for his views on the *state of nature*: human life is "nasty, brutish and short."

*Utilitarianism* is similar to *Realism*. Rather than focusing on preserving power, however, it focuses on the maximum good for the majority. Like Realism, Utilitarianism does "whatever works" but its reference point is the maximum good for the maximum number. Utilitarian thinkers like John Stuart Mill (1645-

1707) and Jeremy Bentham (1748-1832) sought to determine right action through an "ethical calculus". An example of a contemporary Utilitarian philosopher is Peter Singer (1946- ).

Another school of ethical thought was begun by Georg Wilhelm Friedrich Hegel (1770-1831). Hegel believed the ongoing history of thought about Ethics provided a reference point for the field. Hegel realized that every possible ethical system already existed. Left with no options for expansion, he posited that as history progressed humans got closer and closer to determining what was right. Hegel assumed that, through history, humans learn from the past and gradually progress in ethical thought. Karl Marx (1818-1883) and Friedrich Engels (1820-1895) applied Hegel's assumption of progress to politics and economics in *The Communist Manifesto*.

Nineteenth-century philosophers Frederick Nietzsche (1844-1900) and Soren Kierkegaard (1813-1855) did not begin schools of Ethics, but their thought on Ethics was influential nonetheless. Nietzsche argued in *Beyond Good and Evil* that Plato invented notions of *good* and *evil*. Nietzsche believed efforts to determine the good were simply pursuit of a phantom. Although Nietzsche erred in his evaluation of Plato (ideas of good and honor abound in Greek classics such as *The Odyssey*), his ethical ideas gained great prominence in the twentieth century.

Kierkegaard believed in the existence of good and evil, but he challenged the Enlightenment project of finding a system and reference point for determining that good. In *Fear and Trembling*, Kierkegaard uses an event from the biblical story of Abraham (in which God tells Abraham to sacrifice his son Isaac[1]) to argue that a

---
[1] Genesis 22

rational system for deciding ethics may not exist. Kierkegaard particularly opposed Hegel's ethics, which he claimed, behind the smoke and mirrors, was a rational system based on the reference point of *the world spirit.*

There is of course overlap among the various Ethical schools and some philosophers combine schools of thought. A prime example is John Locke (1632-1704). Locke drew from the divine law, Utilitarianism, and Realism to write *A Treatise of Civil Government,* which greatly influenced the drafting of the United States Constitution.

Up to this point, I have only mentioned ethical systems from Western thought. Entirely different ethical systems exist in Asia, the Middle East, South America, and Africa. Ethical thinking, in these continents' cultures, is influenced by their cultures' respective religions, including Hinduism, Buddhism, Taoism, tribal lore, and Confucianism. An important difference between current Western ethical thought and the ethical thought of other cultures, especially those in Asia, involves views on the primacy of the individual (a higher view of the individual exists in the West).

Although the history of thought about Ethics involves thinkers and ideas, what the different systems have in common is that they all try to determine what is *good*. Enlightenment thinkers could not rely on the divine law or other unverified means of defining the good, so they had to come up with a definition or system which defined their reference point for Ethics. Hegel may seem like an exception, but his system was essentially an amalgamation of different reference points. Vital to his system was the assumption that humans got better at defining the good as they progressed through history.

The idea that humans simply progressed in thought was common to other areas of knowledge during Hegel's time. While we obviously do learn from the past, the success of any discipline, as we saw in Chapter Five, ultimately depends on its reference point. The Scientific Revolution did not happen primarily because people learned from the past, but because its reference point, the magical ontological watch, was refined to become the mechanical ontological watch. The assumption that humans progress in thought through history depends entirely upon having a reliable reference point or basis of knowledge. In the same way, Hegel's system depended upon humans progressing in their definitions of the good.

It is impossible to provide a comprehensive or even a basic summary of the history of just Western ethical thought in a single chapter. The chapters on Ontology and Epistemology could be labeled basic summaries, but this chapter on Ethics cannot begin to make such a claim.[2] Because of spatial constraints I will focus on the thought of two philosophers who represent important junctures in the history of Western ethical thought: Aristotle (384–322 BCE) and Immanuel Kant (1724–1804 CE).

Aristotle's famous ethical text is the *Nicomachean Ethics*, which begins with the words, "Every art and every inquiry, and similarly every action and pursuit, is thought to aim at some good; and for this reason the good has rightly been declared to be that at which all things aim." Aristotle did not precisely define this good but he believed that in regard to human action, the reference point was contented individuals like himself and ultimately the contented

---

[2] For a good summary of Western Ethics, I recommend Alasdair Macintyre's *A Short History of Ethics* (London: Routledge Classics, 2002).

Greek city. Contentment is of course subjective, but it generally refers to the overall success and longevity of a city or person.

For Aristotle, the Greek city dweller was the highest form of human life while the Barbarians, who lived outside of Greece, were the lowest. Different levels of human life existed within the Greek city. The lowest consisted of slaves and women, the highest of male masters and philosophers. Although women were condemned to remain low, males could move up and down the rungs of the social ladder. Aristotle's egotistical view of himself has led some thinkers to label him a chauvinist bigot, but in Aristotle's time, most Greeks, including women and slaves, accepted this view of humanity.

Two millennia after Aristotle, Kant was living a happy and contented life in Königsberg, Prussia (now Kaliningrad, Russia). However, he did not use himself or any city as a reference point for Ethics. For Kant, the reference point for the good was *rationale* or reason. In order to test the rationality of any action, Kant developed the *categorical imperative*. The categorical imperative tests the rightness of an action or non-action by requiring a person to first imagine that the action is performed universally by all people. In considering the consequences of universal application of the law, one can evaluate its rationality. For example, to test the rationality of lying, I should consider a world in which everyone lies and ask whether I would want to live with the consequences.

At first glance it can seem that Aristotle and Kant hold similar views on Ethics. Kant's categorical imperative does have parallels with Aristotle's contented and successful city. Aristotle himself asserted that some actions, such as murder and adultery, were simply wrong and not in congruence with a successful city. But while parallels can be made between Kant and Aristotle, a critical difference between their systems exists.

The fundamental difference between Immanuel Kant and Aristotle lies in how they understood human *freedom*. Freedom is the ability of humans to choose their own paths and actions. Because of this freedom, humans are held *accountable* for their actions. Freedom is important to Ethics because without it, Ethics ceases to exist. If humans are all preprogrammed robots, they can never be held accountable for their actions.

All governments and authorities must deal with human freedom. The fact that humans can choose their own path means that their behavior can be unpredictable and possibly hard to manage. The important question all governments face is how they will view and manage human freedom. Human freedom can be seen as a threat, as in dictatorships, whereas in democracies it can be seen as a privilege.

Aristotle assumed that humans acted towards the good which was, in essence, acting towards the overall success of the city and its citizens. There were exceptions, of course, and the task of the city was therefore to train up children from birth to work towards the good of the city and to prevent any misconstrued ideas of the good. For Aristotle and Plato, an important part of raising successful citizens was the instilling of *virtues* to help them move toward the good.

Aristotle believed unchecked passions within the human soul caused humans to develop these misconstrued ideas of the good. Aristotle did not define exactly what passions were, but he saw them generally as mysterious tendencies originating from the soul. Passions were not inherently bad, as the passion for victory and honor on the battlefield suggested, but these passions needed to be combined with virtues such as courage, wisdom, and temperance for an army to actually win a battle. A passion to create wealth is noble, but this must be combined with temperance to prevent the passion turning into greed. By combining a desire like creating wealth with temperance, a person can move toward contentment and the success of the city.

In Aristotle's view, the *virtues* enabled a person to live what is known as the *golden mean.* Instilling virtues in a city's citizens helped them to keep their passions in check and lead balanced lives. Aristotle divided virtues into two groups: *character* virtues and *intellectual* virtues. Character virtues, which functioned to hold the passions in check, included temperance, courage and endurance. Intellectual virtues related to gaining skill and knowledge and included practical wisdom, intuitive reason, and ability in the arts (medicine, arts of war, law and trades). These virtues enabled citizens to become more useful to the city through the acquisition of skills and abilities. Character virtues combined with intellectual virtues directed citizens toward the good and the overall success of the city.

During the Age of Enlightenment, Kant and many other philosophers were not willing to assume that humans acted toward the good. In fact, the ethical systems of Hobbes and Machiavelli suggested that humans by default acted toward the bad and destabilized the state. Because virtues and passions were somewhat mysterious, the philosophers of the time could not include them in their ethical thought. The task of ethical thought was to rationally determine the law code best guaranteed to ensure good behavior and the success of the city.

For Kant, *reason* determined the good, not the path of the contented human. In Kant's view, a human should in no way assume that he or she will do good. He or she should first test his or her actions with the categorical imperative. Kant hoped to formulate a universal law code for all people.

To review, then, Kant saw the good as a formulated law code found through reason, while Aristotle saw the good in the natural motion of a successful citizen towards the success of the city.

Implicit in Kant's and other philosophers' systems was a distrust of human action and an avoidance in trying to understand human action. For Kant, the laws of human freedom posed an unsolvable mystery. The unpredictable motion of humans, influenced by passions and desire, was beyond reason. In establishing his reference point for Ethics, therefore, Kant did not believe understanding human motivation was a factor. For Kant, humans simply needed a legal code, decided by reason through the categorical imperative.

There are several problems with Kant's categorical imperative (one being the extremely difficult task of determining the consequences of all potential actions), but the biggest limitation was addressing this question: *why* should people do the good (or the rational) thing to begin with? It is one matter to formulate a law code, but it is another to make people obey it.

The key assumption upon which Kant depended was that humans *ought* to obey the universal law and follow the categorical imperative irrespective of their desires or motivations. To illustrate Kant's view, imagine a person with a bloody axe knocks on your front door and asks for the whereabouts of your friend. By telling the axe-man where your friend is, there is a good chance that he or she will die. According to Kant, your desire for your friend to live should not come before telling the truth. Truth-telling is verified by the categorical imperative. There is no guarantee that telling the truth will lead to your friend's death, so you are on higher moral ground if you tell the axe-man the truth. According to Kant, desires and passions should not override doing what is right—or what has been determined to be right through the categorical imperative.

Human desire and motivation enables humans to be free, but at the same time it causes them to act unpredictably. Kant did not distrust human freedom in the same way that Hobbes or Machiavelli did, but he did not deal with unpredictability because he did not include human desire and motivation in his Ethics discussions. Unpredictable human motion created problems for Kant's overall philosophical system, as we shall see later; moreover, human freedom proved to be mysterious and beyond human reason.

An unfortunate product of the Age of Enlightenment was an intolerance for mysteries. If something could not be explained it either did not exist or had to be boiled down until it could be explained. Newton's explanation of the mystery of the heavenly bodies' motion filled thinkers of the time with confidence. It was believed that all "mysteries" inherited from the dark ages could be similarly explained.

The Age of Enlightenment aimed to shed light on superstitions and mysteries of the past which kept humans in fear. Mysteries were to be explained or shunned. In theology, the mystery of the Eucharist needed to be solved. It did not make sense that wine and bread taken at the Lord's supper could at the same time be Christ's blood and body. Some other explanation was needed. In Ethics, the mystery of human motivation did not compute. Thus it was avoided. The mystery of being human was dulled or avoided throughout the Age of Enlightenment.

Fundamentally, what it means to be human *is* a mystery. To believe that humans are simply advanced animals is to ignore much of human behavior. Humans are the only beings on earth who wear clothes; they do this not only to keep warm and express themselves, but to cover nakedness. Humans aren't content to live in caves or holes in the ground; rather, they build elaborate houses and spend time and money renovating them. Humans build tall skyscrapers and impressive sports stadiums, sometimes in competition with other humans. In the past humans have labored for hundreds of years to build a single cathedral.

Humans reach for great heights. Humans are land-based, but this does not stop them from taking to the sea and air. Humans reach for something greater than mere survival. They often bypass a multitude of potential partners to pick mates less capable of producing offspring—all because of a mysterious thing called love. Humans are not content watching the same movies or hearing the same songs; they want new films and new music. Humans find it hard to be content with a computer that simply works; they want to design better computers. An alien observer may need a few months to understand the motion of a particular animal, but they would need centuries to understand the mystery of being human.

One aspect of human behavior that an alien observer would immediately notice differs from animal behavior is human sexuality. An alien observer would note that humans want to cover their private parts, while animals have no concern with being naked. An alien observer would also note that there are variations in sexual behavior among humans that are not seen in any animal species.

A survey of 1,571 adults by the *Vancouver Sun* in October 2007[3] showed that 49% of those surveyed had had sex with strangers or people they had just met. Some of the people surveyed had had as many as thirty sexual partners, and 19% had had sexual relations with multiple partners at the same time. Forty percent of those interviewed had had sex with a married person who was not their spouse.

Among the group surveyed, the average age that people began having sex was 18, which suggests that a large group of people were sexually active before that age. The survey by no means comprehends an entire multicultural city like Vancouver, but the results indicate that who one has sex with is a fluid boundary for at least half of those surveyed. The survey also suggests that a large portion of college students are sexually active. Vancouver does not definitively represent the West, but the results of this survey show that variations in sexual behavior exist among humans in the West.

My first experience with sex took place during spring break at Penn State in 1996. I joined a group of friends on a road trip to Montreal, where we stayed with a local one of my friends knew. The goal of the trip was to party, and we did. At a popular nightclub, I started dancing with a girl. I ended up going home with her,

---

[3] *Vancouver Sun*, A6-7; Saturday October 6, 2007.

and when we arrived at her apartment there was no confusion about the agenda for the evening.

I woke up in her bed the next morning; we had breakfast together and after a brief walk said our farewells. This was the first time I had had sex, but the way she went about everything suggested it wasn't hers. What is fascinating about our encounter was that she spoke French and knew very little English. I spoke English and knew absolutely no French. Our communication essentially took place through gesture.

But in a world of contraceptives and the morning-after pill, does it really matter what we think about consensual sex? If two people have a one-night stand, contraceptives can be used to avoid pregnancy and the transfer of disease, and both parties can experience pleasure. Surely this is a good ethical choice. No harm is done and both parties are better off for the experience.

In the above example, I saw sex as a good experience without negative consequences and therefore a good action. My views of right and wrong as regards sexual behavior were based on what I thought was a good experience. The problem with my view, however, is that an experience that *feels* good may not in fact *be* good for you. Taking hard drugs may feel good, but ultimately it is physically harmful.

Our thoughts on the Ethics of sexual behavior ultimately stem from our views about what having sex means. There is of course a legal code under which we operate, but this still leaves us with many options. In discussions about sex, side effects are usually restricted to biological issues because sex is viewed as a purely biological act. But is there more to sex than fluid exchange and momentary pleasure? Our answer to this question hinges upon our ideas about the meaning of sex.

The phrase 'to have sex' can refer to oral sex, anal sex, or vaginal sex. These experiences are by no means equivalent, and a meaningful discussion of each would require more than a solitary chapter in this book. In looking at the question of sexual ethics, I will limit my discussion to vaginal intercourse between a man and a woman. I am also limiting consensual sex to unpaid sex, in which no financial exchange takes place directly because of the sex act.

A great deal has already happened before a man and woman engage in sex. To be naked before a member of the opposite sex is no small thing. Nakedness is not just about wearing no clothes; it is also about the other party or parties who see a person's nakedness. In the West, a person is typically considered naked when his or her private parts are visible to other people. If a person displays a naked foot or hand they are not considered naked, but if a person's genitals are displayed, they are. Nakedness also includes the display of the breasts for women and the display of the buttocks for both sexes. While many naked and topless beaches exist, these are exceptions and not the norm.

For some reason the display of different body parts carries different meaning in various parts of the world. In the Middle East and parts of Asia, the display of the head means something very different from the display of the soles of the feet. Display of the head has more honor, whereas display of the soles of the feet is usually considered offensive. In the West, we don't consider the bare foot offensive, but in daily grooming we spend much time and money *displaying* the face whereas we devote our time and money to *covering* our feet.

The reason the display of certain body parts means something has to do with the *essence of being human* or the human soul. In Chapter Three we saw how all physical objects have an associated essence having to do with the unseen inner programming that gives a particular object its form and motion. The collective essence of all physical objects is the world of prime matter Aristotle described as *Metaphysics*. Human beings have essence in the same way that physical objects like rocks have an associated essence.

In simple terms, our essence is what animates us and causes us to move. Humans look and act differently from rocks because human essence is different from the essence of a rock. Rocks move when they are acted upon; humans can move all by themselves. The motion of a rock can be accurately predicted. Predicting the motion of humans is a different matter.

The essence of being human is complex. Humans are *animate beings* who have the ability to choose their own path. Animals are also animate beings but they move only in a *causal* and predictable manner. Humans have the ability to move *non-causally* because they can think and evaluate their actions (through reflective consciousness). Animals eat when they need to; humans can elect to fast and decide there are certain things which, though edible, they are not going to eat.

Human ability to move non-causally means we are considered free and therefore held accountable for our actions where animals are not. If humans were simply an advanced kind of animal there would be no need for a legal system. The legal system exists because certain actions or non-actions by humans can harm other people (or animals and the environment), and one of the tasks of the court is to establish if a person freely chose to cause harm.

Human essence accounts for our consciousness, passions, talents, desires, motivations, and much more. Our essence works in conjunction with the mind and body to make us who we are. Human essence accounts for our more mysterious qualities and for the inner workings of our body. The causal motion of our inner workings enables the study of medicine and results in humans being somewhat predictable in actions related to their need for food and shelter.

As we go through life we learn more and more about our individual essence, a process known as *actualization*. This accounts for our *identity* or idea of who we think we are and includes our culture, family and friends. However, who we are as an *individual* is primarily related to our own essence. Our particular essence accounts for our unique desires, talents and abilities, and we learn more about our uniqueness as we progress through life. Relationships, activities, and education are important aspects of the actualization process: through them, we find out who we are as individuals.

While males and females have physical and essential differences, they also have physical and essential similarities. The essential similarities in males and females accounts for our *human nature*, or the similar ways in which all humans act and move. Human nature includes our causal nature, but it also includes our desire or passion for wealth, fame, beauty, and justice. To desire beauty and justice assumes a prior understanding of these ideas;

they are thus also linked with our essence.

Perhaps one of the most important human desires is the desire for *relationships* with other humans. Relationships enable humans to take care of basic needs such as food and shelter, but the need for relationship is deeper than satisfying basic needs. As humans we have an innate desire to know and be known by other humans. This desire is beyond rationale or logic. Within our nature is a desire to reveal who we are to others and, conversely, to find out who other people are.

As humans we each carry a mystery: our essence or soul. In interpreting that mystery, we actualize and form our identity. The mystery of who we are is vast, however, and a lifetime is not sufficient for understanding it. This mystery of who we are includes what it means to be part of a culture, a community, and a family, but it also includes what it means to be male or female and who we are as individuals. Who we are as an individual and who we are as a male or female are intricately related, so a basic understanding of both is important in our actualization.

In our desire to know and be known we face a problem. As humans we are *veiled* to one other. In other words, we can't instantly know a person just by looking at him or her. Instead, we must spend time interacting. In this way we build up an idea of what he or she is like. Conversely, he or she builds up an idea of what we are like. In this process of mutually being known, humans form relationships. By nature veiled, we can reverse this state through mutually *unveiling* ourselves through relationship.

The way humans unveil themselves or share knowledge is different from, say, a network of computers. Any group of computers can be networked, providing unlimited access to each other, in a matter of hours. A group of humans is not so easily connected. Some people within a group may simply refuse to share any information with certain others. People are difficult to network because humans can only develop intimacy through mutually revealing knowledge of themselves, and some are by nature reluctant to do this.

Intimacy with another person includes many aspects. It is reflected in the amount of time spent together, activities done together, access to each others' home and family, and eating together. What defines intimacy, however, is mutual knowledge of each other. It is because of this necessity that we can live with other people but still not be intimate with them.

Gaining knowledge of a person happens through communication and, significantly, through *interpreting* that person. This interpretation may be of how he or she moves, how he or she says things, or how he or she looks. Correctly interpreting people and sharing knowledge builds intimacy.

Although our nature is to know and be known we don't want to be fully known to everyone. Humans only want to be intimate with people they like or for whom they have an affinity. In the same way that we like certain books and movies better than others, we like certain people more than others. There are films we watch over and over; similarly there are certain people we want to see again and again. Liking a person is usually a prerequisite to intimacy, but liking a person is not equivalent to being intimate with that person.

It is unclear why we like certain people more than others,

but this mystery ultimately relates to who we are as individuals. Our favorites films and favorite people are important to our actualization because our choices in these areas reflect who we are as individuals. We watch a film repeatedly because something about it intrigues and energizes us. Similarly, certain people intrigue and energize us more than others. Our DVD collection and friends don't definitively sum up the mystery of who we are, but they do say something about who we perceive ourselves to be. As we grow up and actualize these selections can change.

In the same way that we desire intimacy with those we like, we reject intimacy with those we don't like. Revealing knowledge of ourselves builds intimacy. To control intimacy with people, we regulate the knowledge of ourselves that we reveal to others. Regulating knowledge about ourselves can relate to the amount of knowledge we share, but it primarily relates to the fact that certain knowledge reveals more about us than other knowledge.

When I go out on a first date I don't begin by giving my romantic interest a full account of my high school computing class. Rather, I tell her what I like and appreciate. Through sharing these details, I reveal knowledge which says more about who I am than stories about high school. In this way, we prioritize knowledge about ourselves by identifying which details reveal the most about us as individuals. High-priority knowledge includes our personal desires and dreams; it can also include secrets from our life story only known by a few people. By sharing higher-priority knowledge we increase intimacy. By only sharing lower-priority knowledge, we can restrict it.

In the same way that we regulate intimacy through the

knowledge we reveal about ourselves, we regulate intimacy through the veiling and unveiling of our bodies. Our essence and our bodies are intricately connected. Just as information about us reveals something of who we are, our bodies reveal aspects of our selves. Because the different parts of our body have different abilities, each part reveals different things about us. Our mouth communicates information, so it is viewed in a relational way. Our feet stabilize and support our bodies; they are viewed in a functional way.

Because the bodies and essences of males and females are different, sexual attraction exists. Sexual attraction is related to the desire for beauty, intimacy, and procreation, but it begins with the otherness of the male or female. Sexual attraction is desire for the mystery of the other. Physical differences between males and females reflect the different natures of the sexes, and these natures make up the mystery of being male or female.

The otherness of the opposite sex reveals the needs of the different genders for one another. The most obvious is the need to propagate, but these needs also relate to the opposite gender's different nature. The female may be attracted to a strong and secure male, qualities symbolized by a strong physical appearance and confident persona. This need is related to procreation, but it may also stem from a woman's desire for security and strength. The male may be attracted to a sensitive and nurturing female, qualities symbolized by a weaker and softer bodily appearance. While also related to procreation, this need may relate to a man's desire to share weaknesses and insecurities.

It is because male and female bodies reveal different natures that private parts are covered. Our private parts reveal intimate things about us, and even amongst members of the same sex we may wish to cover them. Because the mystery of each other—males and females—is veiled or hidden, it is important to cover the parts which most reflect that mystery.

In the sexual relationship, however, it is natural for a man and a woman to be naked before each other; it is also natural to touch and feel each other's bodies. In the sexual act full bodily access is granted. Such access is natural because of the prior relational access the man and woman have given each other. The sex act symbolizes and reflects this openness. Although males and females are most veiled to each other, in the sexual relationship two humans can be most known to each other. This is the mystery of sex.

But what happens when a man and woman who hardly know each other have sex? They have granted each other full bodily access, but their relational access is lacking. A large discrepancy exists between relational intimacy and bodily intimacy.

A large discrepancy between relational and bodily intimacy is a problem in sexual relationships because the relational connection between body and soul is hardwired into our own being. In having sex with a person who one barely knows, that person is acting in a manner which is diametrically opposed to their essential core.

Sex without intimacy is a violation of the intrinsic connection between a person's soul and body. When a large discrepancy between bodily and relational intimacy develops, a person will naturally try to correct it.

One way to solve the discrepancy is to mentally build up the relationship with the other person, reconciling bodily and relational intimacy. Imagining an intimate relationship is, however, impossible because this always involves extensive mutual sharing. The only other solution is to mentally diminish the relational nature of the other's body. Through diminishing the relational nature of the other's body, bodily intimacy and relational intimacy are apparently reconciled. Bodily intimacy has been brought into line with relational intimacy.

But in the process of diminishing the relational nature of the other's body, that person and ultimately that gender, is dehumanized because a human's essence and body are intricately related. A person may try to deny the connection between body and soul but it is present at a metaphysical level and will always be assumed in themselves and other humans.

The net result of sex without relational intimacy is the dehumanization of the other person—and ultimately the other gender. The other person and gender becomes a non-relational being with a non-relational body used solely for personal pleasure. Since each gender shares the mystery of being human, the dehumanization of the other gender transfers back onto the male or female doing the dehumanizing and causes the man or woman to be disconnected from his or her essence.

A sexual relationship without relational intimacy results, then, in the warping of a person's interpretation of his or her own essence. To accommodate what is happening in the sexual relationship the man and woman dehumanize the other and this ultimately transfers back onto the man or woman who is doing the dehumanizing. Through separating sex from relational intimacy, the process of actualization is corrupted—the process which enables a person to know oneself is handicapped or blocked.

An unfortunate result of the sexual revolution is the assumption that free love and contentment correlate. Technological advances have reduced the biological effects of free love but not the emotional fall out. The West's free love ethic leads the genders to dehumanize each other and causes men and women to disconnect from their essence. Ultimately free love creates alienation, disconnection, and dehumanization; viewing pornography (in 2007, a $6 billion-dollar industry in the US[4]) has similar effects.

In areas such as this Kant's system comes up short. There is no capacity in Kant to consider the human soul or essence and its connection with the body. Kant was concerned with the consequences of action. But the effect of viewing pornography on the human soul is simply out of his bounds. For Kant, *anthropology*, or what it meant to be human, could not determine whether an action is good. The good could only be determined by examination of the act's universal consequences.

I mentioned earlier that human freedom created problems for Kant. In particular, he found it difficult to reconcile human freedom with his explanation of reality. If you recall Chapter Five, Kant had to explain causality and universals to keep modern philosophy going.

John Locke could not solve the problem of universals because he got bogged down in trying to separate universals and particulars. But a more serious problem for Kant was David Hume's denial of causality. Hume believed causality was humans' ability to

---

[4] *The Economist*, "Hard Times." September 12, 2009. 53.

learn from experience, but this did not account for causality itself. The fact that things move predictably is a *result* of causality, *not* an explanation of it. In the shadow of Isaac Newton's discoveries, Kant knew there was a pressing need for an explanation.

The solution came with Kant's Copernican Revolution. While Kant believed in independently existing objects, he knew that these objects also existed as sensations within our head. In other words, our experience of the world out there is registered in our brains through our senses. Kant realized he could still believe in the existence of independent objects while explaining their causal motion through *a priori* knowledge. Given that humans are born with ideas such as beauty and justice, Kant reasoned, they are also born with *a priori* knowledge or inner programming which moves our sensations of real objects in a causal way.

This *a priori* knowledge became known as the *divine consciousness*. Collectively, it accounted for both universals and causality. In addition to divine consciousness, which dealt with pure reason or causality, Kant theorized an *individual consciousness* dealing with practical (or human) reason. Practical reason dealt with human thinking and perception; pure reason is causality itself. Within each human the divine and individual consciousnesses coexisted. The divine consciousness explained causality and universals.

To illustrate Kant's system, think of a modern computer game such as *Rome: Total War*. Players build up the Roman Empire by conquering and governing Barbarian lands. Although the world of the Roman Empire looks real, its objects are ultimately a collection of pixels on a computer screen moved by a program somewhere on the hard drive. The horses and centurions may have corresponded to real objects at one point, but now they are arrangements of pixels moved by a program. In the same way that this program moves Barbarian hordes toward my cities, Kant's *a priori* consciousness in our heads moves the objects that we sense.

Kant's explanation does viably explain causal reality. Using the human brain as a reference point, he explains causality and universals. Kant's philosophical system, however, cannot explain the *non-causal* movement of humans. Divine consciousness or pure reason only deals with causal motion; Kant needed more programming or another level of consciousness which moved humans *non-causally*.

Aside from the difficulty (or impossibility) of introducing non-causal programming (programs are by nature causal, even advanced AI), Kant realized that for humans to be held accountable for their actions, they had to have the ability to move by themselves—with freedom. Other humans not only had to have an independent existence, they had to *move* independently. Therefore their motion could not be accounted for by an inner conscience. Rogue Barbarian hordes committing atrocities against my legions in *Rome: Total War* cannot be prosecuted in a court of law because: a) they are not real people; and b) the Barbarians did not move independently. They were ultimately programmed to move by someone else.

By bringing the motion of objects inside the human head, Kant inadvertently brought in the motion of other humans who could no longer be held accountable for their actions. To solve this problem Kant created a *two-fold metaphysic*. This system separated the motion of the world of objects into the *laws of nature* and the *laws of freedom*. In essence, Kant explained the world using two different philosophical systems. One system dealt with causal motion of objects, the other with non-casual human motion.

The inevitable problem with holding two philosophical systems that explain the same reality lies in explaining how the systems come together. Kant's two systems cannot work simultaneously because they make different assumptions about reality. One assumes *all* objects, including humans, are moved by the divine consciousness; the other (laws of freedom) assumes some objects, namely humans, move by themselves.

If the two systems cannot work simultaneously, perhaps they switch on and off intermittently. But this also poses a dilemma. For example, if a person robs a bank, he can only be held accountable if the laws of freedom apply during the robbery. But Kant's laws of freedom do not account for universal causality because this is a separate philosophical system. If the robber is to be held accountable, the causal motion of the planets and the universe would have to stop or go awry during the robbery.

Ultimately Kant's two-fold metaphysic was a band-aid masking a serious problem with his philosophical system. Unpredictable human motion forced Kant into a corner with regard to his explanation of reality. Kant's only options were to start over or to explain reality using two different philosophical systems.

The idea of Kant's two-fold metaphysic persists into the present day. Today, there are philosophers devoted to Ethics and philosophers devoted to explaining reality. Such division implicitly recognizes the fact that no modern philosophical system has adequately accounted for *causality*, *universals,* and *human freedom.* Kant's system represents the best attempt to explain these three phenomena. Philosophers after him such as Jean-Paul Sartre (1905-1980) needed to redefine causality to make their philosophical systems work.

Believing Kant had solved causality and universals, modern philosophy soldiered on through the likes of Schopenhauer, Nietzsche, and Husserl. I will say more about these philosophers, particularly Heidegger and Sartre, in Chapter Nine. Back in Atlanta, Georgia, Nate and I were only concerned about solving our transportation problem. We headed off to check out the mystery vehicle on the farm.

# CHAPTER 8

## *California Dreaming*

Saying it looked like it had been around the block a few times was an understatement. The car, a Volkswagen Beatle whose paint had long ago been eaten through by the weather, was a rough, rusted–metal color. It had enormous back tires and a large exhaust pipe which protruded about a foot from the back at an upwards angle.

It was hard to believe the car actually worked. Nate and I were speechless. The Bug looked like it would have difficulty getting us back to the gas station, let alone around the United States. But given that it was our only option—and refusal to drive it might offend the mechanics—we gave it a try. If anything, we thought, it would make for a funny story.

With nothing to lose, we climbed in. Nate started the engine, put The Bug into gear, and away we went. Driving around the field, we began to see the humor in our predicament.

"Well, what do you think?" Nate said as we bumped up and down through the green field.

"Let's just say it looks pretty rough," I said.

The upholstery was virtually non-existent. Embedded dirt, large cracks, and sun damage were evident throughout the vehicle. Exposed wires ran up and down the interior, and a blank space gaped where the radio used to be. To top everything off, the windscreen was neatly divided in two by a large crack down the middle.

The fact that the car had made two laps of the field surprised us. Even more surprising was how well it ran.

"Brett, call me crazy, but I think this might work for us," Nate said.

"Yeah, it seems to run pretty good."

After another lap of the field, Nate began to get excited. "This is awesome, man. I think this car actually runs better than The Bus."

Although The Bug was the roughest car I had ever seen, it was a mechanical masterpiece. The mechanics who owned it didn't care much about The Bug's appearance, but they were very interested in its engine and inner workings. Apart from some loose wires, it ran like a dream.

By the time Nate brought The Bug to a stop, both of us were converts. We acquired The Bug for $300 in cash and the broken-down Bus; I paid the $300 and Nate paid The Bus. After signing some registration papers, the trip was back on! In the space of five hours we'd witnessed the death of The Bus—and our trip—only to have our adventure resurrected by The Bug. With Nate at the wheel, we found ourselves back on the highway heading west.

"This is awesome, man," Nate said. "One minute The Bus dies and the next we're driving to California. I love that crack down the windscreen, the bare wires...I just love it!"

Driving a '69 Bus reduced our prospects with women; the Bug took us lower still. The Bug's appearance demanded a response, and we got many during the journey. I knew that Nate was still grieving the death of The Bus, but The Bug had so much character that it managed to partially fill the void. Events like this brought Nate and I closer together. We were different in many ways, but the sheer ridiculousness of our adventure formed an enduring bond between us.

A few days before we left Atlanta, we had another bonding experience while camping out in the forest. Close to our campsite was a river. We decided to do some night swimming. A bridge crossed the river, enabling cars to move in both directions. At nighttime, however, there was very little traffic. When it got dark, we left our tent and headed towards the river. It was a short walk, and we made it with only a few minor scratches from the foliage.

That evening, the stars were shining and except for the

sound of the occasional cricket, all was quiet. We stripped and slid into the river. I kept my underwear on just in case, but Nate left all his clothes on the bank. The water was initially cool, but after a few minutes we were comfortable. It was hard not to enjoy the quiet summer night.

"I told you this would be fun," Nate said, gliding through the water.

"It's great; I can't believe how quiet it is," I said, floating face up in the water.

After a little while, Nate began to get ambitious.

"Hey, man, I think we can make it to the other side; it's not far."

"It's a good paddle, but I guess we've got the whole night," I said.

A confident swimmer, I was keen to join Nate on this venture. And so the late night river crossing began. We were in no hurry to get across so we waded, floating on our backs and taking in the moon and stars. Although it was 200 meters or so across the river, it took us a while because of our leisurely pace. Freestyle would have been more efficient, but we were happy to go as we were.

By the time we reached the other side it felt like we had been swimming for an hour. We beached ourselves on the riverbank to rest and savor our accomplishment. There was not a soul in sight nor sound to be heard.

"I guess we should think about getting back across," I said after ten minutes or so. I was getting cold.

"I don't know about doing that swim again; that took it out

of me," Nate said. "Why don't we walk back across the bridge? I haven't seen a car for ages."

"It's your call, Nate; you're the naked guy."

True, I was taking a risk myself, but we really were in the middle of nowhere and the night was so still. The chances of anyone seeing us were remote at best. And so the late night bridge crossing began. The bridge, paved and smooth, was easy to walk on with our bare feet. We stayed close to the white railing on the right side, and as we neared the halfway point, it seemed our minor gamble had paid off.

"See, man, I told you we'd be fine," Nate said. "Nothing like walking across a bridge completely naked."

A moment later the night sky became strangely illuminated. We couldn't hear anything, but a light seemed to be shining in the sky. Not long after we heard the sound of an approaching vehicle.

"Hey Nate, I think something's coming," I said, picking up the pace.

"Yeah, no kiddin'! We haven't seen a car cross the bridge all night and now this!"

The sound of the engine grew louder. We were facing a close call. "We gotta run, man", Nate shouted. "I'll see you on the other side."

Having no clue what was coming, Nate was off to the races. I was running too. There was nothing honorable about my predicament, but somehow it felt exponentially more shameful to be seen completely naked on that same bridge. Nate was running for his life, his naked frame getting further and further from me. I ran hard too, but short distance sprints were never my forte.

Whatever was coming was getting really close, and I realized I would have to perform a superhuman feat not to be seen. I thought momentarily about jumping off the bridge, but after considering the potential perils I decided I would rather be temporarily embarrassed and live to see another day. The sound of the approaching vehicle grew louder and the bridge filled with light. I slowed to a walk, trying to look like it was normal to take a midnight stroll in one's underwear. I could see Nate frantically running, getting ready to make a last gasp dive into some bushes at the end of the bridge.

The vehicle approached and the driver caught sight of me. I wondered how he was going to interpret the situation. The car kept on traveling; it may have even sped up. The moment passed. A white sedan, which could have been an eighties Oldsmobile or Ford, sped toward Nate. Anxious to find out what had happened, I picked up my pace and ran to the end of the bridge where Nate was emerging out of the bushes.

"Did you see me dive, man? I'm a little scratched up but I think I made it," he said, doing a quick assessment of his body.

There was no telling if Nate had been seen or not, but it was better for him to assume he wasn't. All I know is that a naked man diving into some bushes near midnight must have been an unforgettable sight. From the way Nate talked about his dramatic escape, it seemed like he either enjoyed these situations or looked for positives to redeem his predicaments—an ability I appreciated.

After the night's adventures we retired to our tent, dried off, and climbed into our sleeping bags. It took me a while to calm myself, but I eventually settled down and went to sleep. For some reason we didn't talk much about the night's events the next morning. It may have been too hard to believe it all actually happened.

As we motored toward California, Nate and I adjusted to our new vehicle. It seemed darker in The Bug and we were much closer to the road. I preferred the ascetic feel of The Bus, but The Bug was our mode of transport now. The transition meant we had to leave behind a lot of things—the jigsaw puzzle, random flea market artifacts. These items weren't of much practical use, but it was sad to leave tangible memories behind. Nate took the purple Grateful Dead sticker off The Bus and stuck it to The Bug to preserve The Bus' memory. I'm not sure what happened to the Buddha; it probably suffered Nate's wrath for failing to prevent the death of The Bus.

Because The Bug had far less storage space than The Bus, we had to reorganize. In The Bug we had two storage areas: the back seat and the front trunk. The trunk leaked, so in there we stored water resistant items such as camping gear and tools. Everything else ended up in a pile on the back seat. Despite the ascetic downgrade, The Bug was faster and didn't need oil top-ups every two hundred miles. It also ran well, though sometimes one of us would have to jiggle some wires to get the engine to start. Somewhere in The Bug's use as a farm vehicle, it developed a few loose connections. For the most part, this caused no drama—except for the time we were chased out of a Hooters restaurant.

On our first night driving The Bug out of Georgia, we came upon a Hooters in the middle of nowhere. Unlike Odysseus in *The Odyssey*, we made no attempt to resist the temptation.[1] At that time

---

[1] In the Greek epic, Odysseus is warned about sailing past the Sirens. In preparation, he puts beeswax in the ears of his crew and ties himself to the mast to resist the temptation.

I'm not sure if there was a Hooters in Pennsylvania, but there certainly weren't any in Western Australia; this was a first for both of us. I didn't know what to expect; all I knew was that its sexually-charged atmosphere rendered it somewhat forbidden, and that made it worth stopping.

My first impression was more or less that of a normal, slightly dark restaurant. One of the alluring sirens seated us.

"Can I get you two a drink?"

"Yeah, sure, can we each have a coke?" Nate said. The waitress left and Nate filled me in on the strategy. "So the deal here, man, is we order the cheapest thing off the menu and enjoy the women."

A few minutes later the waitress came back and gave us our drinks and menus. Suddenly Nate's delight turned sour.

"What!" Nate exclaimed, "Four dollars for a soda! Man, no way I'm paying four dollars for a soda." Nate liked alluring women, but paying that much for a coke was beyond him. I don't think either of us had touched our sodas. Now they had become forbidden.

"We have to go, man; I didn't realize it would be this expensive." Nate had no option now but to employ his get-out-of-jail-free card, when the waitress returned.

"Excuse me…um…ma'am; we didn't realize it would be so expensive here and…well…he's (referring to me) from Australia. He doesn't know how things work in this country."

I don't know what the poor waitress thought about the whole situation. She was probably equally amused and offended. We unseated ourselves and made for the door. Unsure how the

Hooters management would interpret all this, we thought it best to leave the scene as fast as possible.

"Okay, let's hope The Bug starts up; we need to get out of here quick," Nate said. He turned the key. Nothing happened.

"Brett, you need to get out and shake the wires." Nate was panicking.

I went to the back of the Bug and opened the hood. In the dark, I could barely make out the wires. I fumbled and frantically shook, visions of an angry mob flashing before my eyes. I had a sick sense that our luck had finally run out.

"Keep shaking, man! We gotta go!" Nate shouted. He continued to churn the starter, but my frantic shaking had no effect. Finally, after a moment that lasted an eternity, the engine roared to life.

"Get in, man!" I rose from the gravel, slammed the hood, and scampered into The Bug. As I closed the door, Nate floored it and we sped out of the parking lot to the safe anonymity of the highway. Our heart rates began to slow. We were relieved to be free from potential danger, but both of us had begun to grow weary of such predicaments.

By our second day in The Bug, we were getting accustomed to our new mode of transport. The sun seemed a little brighter and the trees a little greener as The Bug swallowed up miles on the highway. We had to forgo Jimmy Buffet, The Grateful Dead, and The Doors, but with our dream of going out west revived, we weren't all that concerned.

"There's no way we can do Mexico and South America now," Nate mused. "If we take this thing across the border it could be real difficult getting back in. The paperwork's not gonna be finalized until we get home again."

"So what's the plan?"

"Well, I was thinking we could go to Tijuana. It's just south of the border, so we can park The Bug in the States, walk across, and take a cab. What do you think?"

"Well I guess it does solve the paperwork problem, and it gets us to Mexico."

We agreed to spend a few days in Tijuana and keep The Bug stateside. Even if we still had The Bus, it would have been a good decision. As it was, we were minimally prepared for a trip around the U.S., let alone a cross-cultural road trip through Mexico and South America.

On our second night on the road we slept at a rest stop in Arkansas. We found a large tree and unrolled our mats and sleeping bags. As we settled in, we began an acquaintance with the local mosquitoes. After about twenty minutes of high-pitched buzzing and bites, I gave up and returned to the comfort of The Bug's back seat. Miraculously, Nate was able to sleep in spite of the mosquito swarm. His only complaint the next morning concerned a visit from a daddy-long-legs family.

The next day we entered Oklahoma. After lunch we began to notice a change in the landscape. The sun seemed brighter, the sky bigger. We were surrounded by open green fields, and our Georgia "Peach State" license plates drew notice. People waved, wondering how on earth our vehicle had made it all this way.

Later in the day, as the sun began to sink in the west, we found a rest stop. There were no large trees or buildings to conceal us, so we gathered our sleeping gear and marched off into one of the surrounding fields. We climbed over a fence, trudged about a hundred yards through the green stubble, and laid out our mats and pillows. I put my head down and observed the starry heavens above. Before long sleep overcame me.

I awoke to see nothing but blue sky and green fields. I glanced over at Nate; he was awake in his sleeping bag, looking up at the sky. The air was still cool, though the sun was getting brighter and brighter. It was one of the best waking-up experiences of my life.

The rest stops usually didn't provide showers, so whenever we spotted a peaceful river or creek we stopped to wash. Living on the cheap had its disadvantages, but having our daily wash in a river was not one of them. Revived and clean, we jumped back into The Bug and continued our journey.

We passed into Texas mid-morning and saw a sign advertising ultra-cheap gas. As we drove, it became apparent why it was so cheap. It was a ghost town. At some stage it had been full of life and energy, but all that remained were empty buildings, old signs, and gas stations. I found it eerie even in the middle of the day.

As we passed through Texas into New Mexico, the countryside gradually changed, transitioning from green fields to arid desert. Harsh, hardy brush replaced green stubble; flat fields became rocky outcrops. The cool breeze of the previous day was now hot air, and we were feeling it in The Bug.

The emptiness was somewhat unnerving, but it was also cathartic. It allowed my thoughts to wander back to Atlanta and Tony. Tony was hard to forget. Living with him was such a bizarre and interesting experience, and I felt something significant had happened during our time there, something hard to put my finger on. Nate and I fit right in with Tony's friends and lifestyle—we could have spent another month together if Tony hadn't had to leave.

The Bug steadily rolled down the highway under the bright blue sky. Nate had driven all morning; now midday approached. We were planning an all-nighter. Driving through the night enabled us to get out West faster; it was also cooler. I took over the driving a few hours after lunch, and Nate took over after dinner. Later that evening when we stopped for gas, Nate crawled onto the pile in the back to sleep.

"Wake me when we get to Albuquerque, man."

After a few minutes, Nate was fast asleep and it was just me and the open road. The cool night was refreshing. I enjoyed my newfound solitude; Nate was an easy guy to be with, but it was nice to have time alone. After four hours of solitary bliss, we arrived in Albuquerque. I pulled up at a gas station and Nate slowly came to his senses. It was completely dark, and almost no one was around. I paid for the gas and crawled into the back seat, looking forward to a blissful sleep.

"Have a good night, Nate," I said.

"Sure, man; see you tomorrow."

The sound of the engine and the rhythm of the road put me to sleep in a heartbeat. Some of the best sleeps I ever had came on that clothes pile in the back seat of The Bug.

The next thing I knew it was daylight, and we were at a different gas station.

"Nate, where are we?" I said, adjusting to the light.

"We're about four hours from Tucson; we should be there around lunch time."

"How was your night at the wheel?" I asked.

"It was great. Hardly anyone on the road; we made really good progress."

The weather grew noticeably hotter as we progressed through Arizona. Nate, finally willing to dispense with his no-cost accommodation philosophy, found us a cheap hotel where we could recuperate from our long hours of driving. After we checked in, we turned the air conditioner on full blast, laid on our beds, and watched TV.

The next morning we decided to stay another night at the hotel. Nate wanted to get The Bug checked out before we drove through the Rocky Mountains. One of the locals told us about the challenge ahead; the mountains were notorious for killing cars. The long drive coupled with the intense heat caused many a vehicle to overheat or break down; a water tap had been placed every couple of miles to cool overheating engines and provide drinking water. The guy also told us about a Volkswagen garage where we could get The Bug checked out.

Driving across the U.S. gave me a new perspective on the country. The land was incredibly diverse, as were the people. From my previous, limited view of the U.S., I understood it to be a place where you were always in danger and could never trust anyone. In certain parts of the country this is true, but Nate and I had encountered so much generosity that it was difficult to know what to do with my previous assumptions. In almost every predicament, people welcomed strangers and helped those in need.

After we returned from the garage, Nate and I spent the day soaking in the cold air conditioning and relaxing. Our stay at the hotel was an oasis experience after our long trip from Atlanta. Given its apparent condition it was something of a miracle that The Bug had made the distance, but the ascent up the mountain pass would be its biggest test yet.

Early the next morning we rose, got everything packed in The Bug, and began the traverse. We had been advised to start early to avoid the midday heat, and the road was quiet as we began the ascent. Nate down shifted as we roared up the mountain in that most unlikely of vehicles.

Twenty minutes in, there was no sign of The Bug doing anything unusual.

"I don't know if that guy at the hotel was overstating it, but we're doing pretty good here. We're halfway up and The Bug sounds great."

The Bug really was a wonder. People from Oklahoma honked at us when they saw how far The Bug had come—and now it was powering up the Rocky Mountains enroute to Tijuana! By mid-morning The Bug had conquered the ascent. It was all downhill from here.

"We made it, man!" Nate shouted as The Bug headed down the mountain. The ease with which The Bug climbed the mountain was slightly anti-climactic, but after all the drama we'd experienced so far this was a nice change.

"I can't believe how easy that was. There's no stopping this car," Nate said. The Bug didn't always start when we wanted it to, but once we got it started it just kept on rolling. This reliability led us to nickname it Steady Rollin' Bob Margolin, after the blues guitarist we came across in Atlanta.

After the descent it was full steam ahead towards Tijuana. We arrived at the Mexican border in the early afternoon and found a place to park. We packed our bags with essentials and left everything else on the back seat. The great thing about The Bug was that we didn't have to worry about theft. Setting aside the fact that someone would have to jiggle the wires at the back to get it started, its appearance itself was a security device. No one in the their right mind would think it contained anything of value.

We walked across the border into Mexico and hailed a cab. We arrived in Tijuana late in the afternoon and found a cheap hotel. Our room was dark and nondescript; Nate and I spent much of our time out and about. The agenda consisted of drinking cheap beer, going to a bullfight, listening to Mexican music, and enjoying Mexican women.

On our first day in Tijuana, we saw the bullfight—a first for both of us. Initially it was exciting to see the matador dodge and weave around the charging bull, but I was disturbed to see that the bull actually got killed during the fight. Having been raised on a farm, I had seen animals die. Death in this manner was harder for me to deal with.

In Tijuana, a large bottle of Tecate beer cost a dollar, and Nate and I went through a few bottles during our two nights there. After the bullfight we sat on the beach, enjoying our surroundings as we drank. There were lots of bars and nightlife, and during my stay I had several sexual encounters with Mexican women.

Living a loose lifestyle was not something I consciously aimed at. If anything, I thought I tended toward the conservative side. I wasn't sure what had happened to me in Tijuana—or even during spring break in Montreal earlier that year. In many ways, sex had become just an experience for self-gratification.

Although I was in a bad place in regard to my sexuality and subsequent view of women, this was not the end of my journey. In the years that followed a process of redemption began that gradually healed the damage I had done to myself. But as you will see later, the beginning of that redemption was not caused by my own doing. Something else at work on this trip seemed to be orchestrating events.

# CHAPTER 9

## *The End of Things*

As Frodo and Sam rest on a hillside overlooking the unknown road ahead, Frodo recalls some traveling wisdom from Bilbo: "It's a dangerous business, Frodo, going out of your door. You step onto the road, and if you don't keep your feet, there is no knowing where you might be swept off to. Do you realize that this is the very path that goes through Mirkwood, and that if you let it, it might take you to the Lonely Mountain or even further and to worse places?"

Frodo and Sam had not heard anything of Bilbo since he literally disappeared from the Shire seventeen years before. During his 111th birthday party, Bilbo concluded his speech with an unemotional "goodbye", slipped on his magical ring, and vanished into thin air. After Bilbo disappeared, Frodo inherited all his possessions, including Bilbo's magical ring.

At the time of his inheritance Frodo was thirty-three. For the next seventeen years, he lived at Bag-End, the property tended by his friend Samwise Gamgee. Bilbo had many treasures stored up at Bag-End (including a vest of Mithrail worth more than the Shire itself), but one of these treasures, Bilbo's magical ring, held far more significance than Bilbo or Frodo ever imagined.

Bilbo and Frodo are both actors in the larger story of Middle Earth. Even though Bilbo and Frodo are ignorant of the larger story, or *Metanarrative,* of Middle Earth, they and all other hobbits are inextricably caught up in it. Only when Gandalf explains the story of Middle Earth does Frodo realize the importance of The Ring and his peril staying in the Shire.

The Ring was made in the Second Age of Middle Earth, long before the Shire existed. Part of a series of rings made by the elves during a time of renaissance on Middle Earth, these rings bestowed special powers upon their keepers, prolonging life and warding off the decays of time. Sauron, servant of Melkor and Dark Lord of Middle Earth, helped the elves make the rings, but in secret he made a ruling ring which could unite and rule the rings and their keepers.

The elves learned about Sauron's plan and fled with the

three most powerful rings. In response, Sauron gave the dwarves seven of the remaining rings. The other nine he gifted to the men of Middle Earth so that he might gain power over them. Unaware of Sauron's plan, the dwarves and men were gradually corrupted.

As corruption of Middle Earth increased, Sauron's power grew. Eventually the men, dwarves, and elves formed the Last Alliance to oppose Sauron. On Dagorlad, the battle plain before the gate of the Black Land, the Last Alliance fought Sauron's minions. They defeated his army and laid siege to Sauron's stronghold, the Dark Tower Barad-dûr. The siege was so fierce that Sauron himself entered the battle, inflicting much damage on the assaulting army and slaying the commanders of the Alliance: Gil-galad and Elendil. But Sauron was thrown down in battle and Isildur, son of Elendil, claimed the master ring from Sauron's hand.

The fall of Sauron and the destruction of Barad-dûr ushered in the Third Age of Middle Earth. Sauron forsook his body, but he was not destroyed. Isildur could have cast the master ring into the fires of Mount Doom, destroying it, but he had grown attached to The Ring and refused. The Ring remained with Isildur until his company was besieged by orcs near the Misty Mountains. Isildur put on The Ring, but it abandoned him during his escape and descended to the bottom of a river. It remained there for almost two and-a-half thousand years.

While The Ring remained lost, Sauron could not overcome the power of the elves, keepers of the three most powerful rings. If Sauron found the ruling ring, the elves would have to abandon their rings, allowing Sauron to reign on Middle Earth; if the ruling ring was destroyed, Sauron would be eternally defeated. The Ring became legend, then passed out of all knowledge. But it was waiting, and in the 2463rd year of the Third Age (862 SR) it was found by a seafaring hobbit named Déagol.

Déagol's friend, Sméagol, murdered Déagol and took The Ring. Sméagol's subsequent corruption led his family to drive him away. Sméagol, who could not bear the light of day, found solace in the dark caves of the Misty Mountains. The Ring consumed him. Sméagol's corruption was such that his physical form diminished, and he changed his name to Gollum. The Ring gave him unnaturally long life, and he dwelt in darkness for almost five-hundred years.

During his first adventure with the wizard Gandalf and the dwarves, Bilbo encountered Gollum in the depths of the Misty Mountains (1341 SR). Bilbo took The Ring from Gollum and, to his amazement, found that he disappeared every time he put it on. Using The Ring, Bilbo evaded Gollum and other dangers during his first adventure. After the slaying of the dragon Smaug, Bilbo brought The Ring back to Bag-End. There it remained for sixty years. Bilbo used it for the last time at his farewell birthday party.

After Bilbo took The Ring from Gollum, rumor grew on Middle Earth that The Ring had been found. Gandalf, in attendance at Bilbo's party, grew suspicious. Though he was a long way from believing Bilbo held the One Ring of Power, after hearing reports that The Ring had been found Gandalf realized he had to act. After visiting Frodo to ensure The Ring's safety, Gandalf dug into the archives of Middle Earth and found an account by Isildur describing The Ring of Power. Isildur recorded its markings as follows:

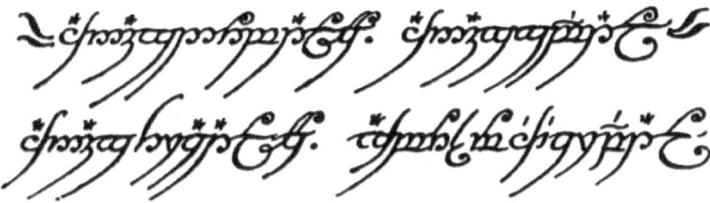

In the language of Mordor, these markings translate as, "One Ring to rule them all, One Ring to find them, One Ring to bring them all, and in the darkness bind them." According to Isildur, the markings become visible only when the ring is heated in fire. Gandalf hastily returns to the Shire and throws the ring into the fireplace at Bag-End. Once the ominous markings become illuminated, the history of Middle Earth takes a sudden turn—along with the course of Frodo's life.

When Gandalf gives Frodo the ominous news about The Ring, Frodo struggles to comprehend this turn of events.

"This ring!" he stammers. "How on earth did it come to me?"

"Ah!" says Gandalf. "That is a very long story. The beginnings lie back in the Black Years, which only the lore-masters now remember. If I were to tell you all that tale, we should still be sitting here when spring has passed into winter."

Gandalf tells Frodo the short version of The Ring's age-long journey from Isildur to Gollum and finally to Bilbo. But Frodo is not simply asking about the story of The Ring. The course of his life being determined by events entirely outside his control perplexes him. If Bilbo had never found The Ring, Frodo would never have had to deal with it. If Isildur had destroyed it at the beginning of the Third Age, The Ring and Sauron would only be subjects of history.

Events that took place thousands of years before Frodo came into existence cause him to flee the Shire with his gardener Sam. In ordinary circumstances, Frodo would have been, like most other hobbits, content to live his whole life in the Shire and never tread into danger. But the life and story of Frodo and all other beings on Middle Earth is intertwined with the greater history or *Metanarrative* of Middle Earth and the story of The Ring.

In the same way that events thousands of years before Frodo's birth direct his life, the course of our lives are also directed by events beyond our control, some of which took place thousands of years before our birth. As humans, we are not born into a vacuum, but into a reality characterized and defined by ongoing stories. Like Bilbo and Frodo, we may not have a clear understanding of the stories into which we are born, but we are part of them nonetheless.

The concept of events beyond our control affecting our path in life, *contingency,* relates to *Teleology*, the assumption I will discuss in this chapter. The word Teleology originates from the Greek word τελος, which means end (or final). The English word "end" usually refers to the finish or to final events, but it also means purpose or direction. Teleology, while related to final events, is more concerned with purpose. If you recall Chapter Three, *Telos* was one of four causes Aristotle believed characterize everything that exists (final cause).

Teleology is a small word for the wide concept it represents. In Aristotle's time, the idea of final cause and purpose was new and controversial. Plato and other contemporary Greek philosophers did not believe individual objects had purpose or direction. For Plato, individual objects did not even count as knowledge. They were shadows and illusions of the greater world of forms. But Aristotle began his philosophy from the assumption that the form and motion of objects could be explained and that individual objects counted as knowledge. Aristotle believed there was an underlying pattern or order in how things moved, and that the form and motion of objects formed a stable reference point of knowledge.

Aristotle's thought on the natural world was a radical departure from Plato. However, the previously accepted idea that objects in the world of substance could not be explained originated from another Greek philosopher, Parmenides (520-450 BCE), founder of the Eleatic school of philosophy on the east coast of Italy. Parmenides began his thought from what was seen, but he soon confronted the problem of explaining origins. The fact that something was there demanded an explanation of how that thing came to be. Parmenides determined that there were two options.

One explanation argued that the thing came from nothing or non-existence. To even talk about non-existence or nothing was problematic enough, due to the impossibility of defining it, but a still greater problem concerned how a tree or a human being could emerge from nothing. It is one thing for objects to change; it is entirely different for something to come from nothing or for matter to come from non-matter. Parmenides knew that even if he granted that one could talk about nothing or non-existence, it was simply impossible for something to emerge out of nothing.

The fact that no one was able to solve the riddle of something coming from nothing led Parmenides to conclude that it was not possible to explain reality beginning with individual objects. If the mere presence of a thing was unexplainable, it was folly to explain the motion or form of that thing. This led Parmenides to question if individual objects actually existed. He concluded that reality was one elaborate phenomena rather than individually existing objects.

Aristotle was uncomfortable with Parmenides' conclusions. He accepted that one might not know the origin of something, but he felt this did not imply that the thing did not exist. Aristotle did not really prove Parmenides wrong. Rather he believed the assumption that things changed was more fundamental to philosophy than solving the riddle of something coming from nothing. Whatever the origin of a thing, Aristotle believed the task of philosophy was to explain its change and motion. In response to Parmenides' riddle, Aristotle assumed that matter was eternal and that objects had a beginning even if he could not explain their origin.

If the form and motion of individual objects formed a stable reference point of knowledge, Aristotle argued, then each object had to have a final cause or purpose. In other words, if the form and motion of objects were not random but somehow ordered and explainable, each object had to be heading toward a final cause or destination. In this way, Aristotle assumed all objects had an inherit *purpose* or trajectory.

Long before Aristotle, however, humans have thought about purpose. Humans have always had ideas about their desired end and what sort of life they would like to live; they rarely live in this world without hopes and dreams. While much dreaming and hoping in ancient civilizations concerned the afterlife, the ancients also pondered their earthly existence. In Greek thought, each human life was thought to be governed by the Fates; the weaving of events by the Fates determined each human's path. The Greeks, anxious about the uncertainty of life, believed that appeasing the gods could influence fate and enable events to go their way.

Frodo is disturbed and perplexed by Gandalf's news about The Ring because he does not like the consequences of possessing an object whose path determines Middle Earth's fate. If Frodo was ambivalent about the course and direction of his life, Gandalf's news would not trouble him. Why would it matter to Frodo what happens to him or Middle Earth if he feels the same way about all possible outcomes? The Ring concerns Frodo because he had a different end or purpose in mind for his life than the one in which he is suddenly immersed.

As long as humans have lived, we have been concerned and anxious about the course and direction of our lives. The uncertainty associated with contingency has always been a problem. We desire a good outcome, yet that outcome is usually dependant on events and circumstances beyond our control. Although modern Western humans are less likely to consult mediums and appease particular gods like the ancients, we are not content to sit and fall prey to contingency.

As humans, we look to overcome contingency. In the modern world, insurance is one way of dealing with the uncertainty of life; as a result, insurance is a multi-billion dollar industry. On a more personal level, we look to our own abilities and resources to overcome contingency. Although these measures can be useful in dealing with matters of uncertainty, there are events, for good or for bad, which are simply beyond our control. It is indeed a dangerous business to walk out of one's door.

Further, it is a confusing business. Many paths lead out from our front door, not just the one to Mirkwood. We don't know exactly where each one will take us. While we desire a good outcome, it is difficult to know if the path we have chosen is in fact good.

Through history, humans have confronted two difficult conundrums: working out which path or direction they will head in life, or *Teleology;* and dealing with the fact that their path in life is *contingent* on other events and people they cannot control. As we shall see in this chapter, how we deal with these two conundrums is determined by how we understand ourselves as humans and how we conceptualize the nature of reality.

In Chapter Seven, we encountered the word *good* in respect to ethics and human action. Numerous systems of ethics emerged during the Enlightenment, but fundamentally they were all systems of thought aimed at determining the good. In the case of Immanuel Kant, the reference point for the good was what was rational. This could be found through the categorical imperative. The good for Aristotle was mysterious rather than defined. Aristotle did not construct a reference point for the good like the Enlightenment philosophers. Rather, he viewed the good as teleological in nature. In other words, Aristotle did not believe he had to come up with a definition of the good; he assumed the good was the ultimate purpose and destination of all things, including human action.

Because Aristotle assumed that humans moved toward the good, it followed that the successful and contented Greek city encapsulated his overall idea of the good. Aristotle realized that Greek citizens might not be as high-minded as he was; thus, he believed that the key to developing successful citizens was instilling virtues in them that would enable them to look beyond immediate goods such as accumulating possessions and gaining power. In this way, the citizens could develop virtues and live the golden mean, which balanced the rational and irrational elements of the human soul.

While many goods may exist, Aristotle believed that humans aim at one ultimate good served by all others. To illustrate: in construction, the ultimate good of a finished house is the motivation behind stacking bricks to build it. In building my own house, many good things such as brick-laying, plumbing, and carpentry are involved. They all contribute, however, to the ultimate good: the finished house. For a passerby to say I am laying bricks purely because I like laying bricks would be to miss the obvious motivation—however I feel about stacking bricks, I ultimately laid them to build the house I have in mind.

As a house is built with an ultimate good in mind, so our lives are built. Whatever our idea of the ultimate good, it forms the underlying motivation for all our actions. As humans, we have a unique ability to project ourselves into the future—an ability enabled by our *reflective consciousness*. Reflective consciousness allows us to step back and evaluate our actions, as we saw in Chapter Seven, but it also allows us to plan and bring about our idea of the ultimate good.

However, our idea of the ultimate good may not be a definition of the ultimate good. Rather, it may be an idea of what a good or *contented* life looks like. There are exceptions, of course. For Gollum, the ultimate good is The Ring itself. Possession of The Ring motivates all his actions. Aristotle argued that the more intangible a person's idea of the ultimate good, the better he or she seemed to do in life. The contented life for Aristotle was not owning the good itself but participating in a reflection or emanation of the ultimate good.

For Aristotle, contentment was not a temporary state. Happiness and satisfaction came as someone examined the overall course of his or her life. What it means to live a contented life is of course subjective, varying greatly from person to person. But whatever our idea of the contented life, it is toward this end that we move. It forms the underlying motivation for all our actions.

While varying ideas about the contented life exist, some elements are shared among most people. On a basic level, contentedness is characterized by the presence of essentials such as health, food, water, and shelter. Each is important because it enables us to survive. Today, we call the ongoing presence of these essentials economic security. But humans need more than health, food, water, and shelter to be content—after all, one could dwell alone in a dark dungeon and technically be economically secure.

In addition to material necessities, human contentment is also characterized by healthy relationships with other humans. As we saw in Chapter Seven, humans are relational beings. We desire the mutual revelation of self to others. Such relationships are found in the context of family and friendships. Through these relationships, humans develop a sense of belonging and relational maturity. But economic security and a network of healthy relationships does not guarantee contentment—one could be living in a concentration camp and have these things present.

Another vital element of human contentment, then, is *freedom*. In Chapter Seven, I defined freedom as the ability to pick one's own path. Freedom is an important element of contentment because it allows a human to become who he or she is meant to be—to realize his or her *potential*.

As humans, we all have potential. We are not born into a vacuum; neither are we born as vacuums. Our brains are not equivalent to blank hard drives; rather, we are each born with a pre-existing operating system which can never be erased. This operating system can absorb new programs, but its fundamentals cannot be changed. This pre-existing operating system inside of us forms part of our *essence* and contributes to the mystery of being human.

Realizing one's potential is fundamental to human contentment. At an early age, little boys and girls want to grow up and live the lives of successful adults. They also want to realize their potential as a man or woman. This involves growth and development of physical bodies, but becoming a man or a woman also relates to inner essence, including educational, emotional, and relational development. Gender wars today make the distinction between male and female nature increasingly controversial, but at an essential level men and women are different from each other. Characteristic of masculine essence is a desire to initiate and build, while feminine essence is characterized by a desire to nurture and preserve.

Boys and girls are rarely content to become generic men or women, however. An important part of realizing one's potential is realizing one's potential as an *individual*. What makes us individual begins with our outer appearance and carries through to our essential nature. Within our essential nature, our gifts, abilities, talents, and intricacies reside. Discovery and nurturing of our individual elements enables us to actualize and realize our individual potential.

Our problem as humans is that we are not born with an attached manual outlining our particular talents, abilities, likes, and dislikes. Instead, we discover our unique characteristics through the process of *actualization,* defined in Chapter Seven as the ongoing interpretation of our essence.

To realize our potential as an individual, we have to somehow know who and what we are meant to become. Through the process of actualization, we develop an idea of our potential. Actualization begins from the moment we are born. Our parents and immediate family are our first experience of actualized individuals; through being raised by our parents, we develop ideas of what an actualized human looks like. Our parents and immediate family may carry out their own interpretation of our essence and tell us their interpretations of our abilities, talents, and unique traits.

Our talents and abilities are not perceived in a vacuum, however, but are identified by seeing how we perform in *relation* to other human beings. If a boy's father believes his son is going to be an elite goal tender, the father must know that the boy's ability to stop pucks is significantly better than that of others his age. If a girl's mother believes her daughter is going to be a movie star, then the mother must know her daughter is a noticeably better performer than other girls her age.

Although our parents are important models and guides for us in the process of actualization, they do not define who we are. We are born into this world through our parents, but we are not solely a product of them. Our parents influence who we are, but they do not write out the manual describing all of our talents and intricacies—or even our gender. In order to fully actualize, we must at some point begin to separate from our parents and develop as individuals, a process most evident during adolescence.

By finding out our individual traits and abilities, we progress in actualization. Through the nurturing and development of our talents we become who we are meant to be. Part of the mystery of being human is that, although we grow and change on a daily basis, our essence remains the same. From the moment of our conception to the time of our death, our essence remains constant.

The paradox of life is that while freedom allows us to actualize as individuals, we are not free to be whoever we wish. Our *Telos* as humans ultimately relates to the essence given to us at conception. Through the process of actualization we realize our potential as humans. Through this process we are better able to determine the path we should walk.

But sadly the process of actualization can go awry. Some humans do not reach even an elementary level. Actualization depends on a process of interpretation, and it is possible for a person to make or believe *incorrect* interpretations about his or her essence. The process of actualization is in fact delicate, especially early in life. Children who are victims of child abuse (especially sexual abuse), slavery, or who are led into bad behavior can stop or be inhibited in actualizing because these events diametrically oppose their inner essence.

The most obvious cause for a human failing to actualize is an early death. Most humans in the developed world expect to live eighty or more years, but unfortunately many die earlier than that. Further, living a long life does not guarantee that a person will reach his or her potential—Gollum lived more than five-hundred years and failed to reach his potential as a seafaring hobbit.

Realizing our potential is not just about surviving and living a long life but about steadily progressing in the process of actualization and accurate interpretation of oneself. There are many reasons for the process of actualization going awry. As a result, people do not become who they are meant to be. But fortunately, as humans, we are not without hope. Through the process of *Redemption* we can be healed and become more fully ourselves. I will say more about this in Chapter Eleven: *The Hope of Redemption*.

Becoming who we are meant to be involves knowing and developing our unique traits and abilities, but more fundamentally it concerns knowing what it means to be human. We are all born into this world as humans, in form and essence, and this fact alone has major implications for the actualization process. Although all humans are unique, we share the mystery of being human. Our idea of what this means is vital to our actualization.

In the same way that we discover our unique characteristics in relation to other human beings, we discover what it means to be human through seeing who we are in relation to the world around us. This begins with our immediate family and culture, and takes place more broadly in the context of a space-time reality. As humans, we do not live in a void consisting only of ourselves and other people. Rather, our space-time reality enables our existence. Our idea of how we relate to this reality as humans forms our identity and shapes our idea of what it means to be a human more broadly.

We realize early in life that we need the world to survive. We depend on the world for food, water, and shelter, and thus we need our physical surrounds to maintain suitable conditions for obtaining these basics of survival. Our day-to-day existence on Earth in fact depends on many intricacies particular to our planet, such as a constant axis tilt to regulate the seasons and a specific distance from the sun to regulate the temperature.

At an early age we also realize other beings called animals exist on Earth. We need animals to sustain our existence, and a part of actualization is forming an idea of how we as humans relate to the animals around us. Some similarities are visible between humans and animals, but we also see significant differences between ourselves and even the most advanced animal.

Humans look different from animals, but the biggest difference between us and animals is in their essential natures. As humans, we have a unique ability to move non-causally, an ability made possible by our reflective consciousness. Our ability to stand back from ourselves enables us to actualize and to create, evaluate, and choose our own path through life. Humans also have a highly advanced relational nature, facilitated by our ability to use language, which has important implications for human nakedness and sexuality and our ability to grasp ideas like justice and beauty which far surpasses that of animals.

The gap between humans and animals is indeed vast and sets humans apart. None of humankind's unique and advanced abilities have been seen in any animal of the past or present. Whatever one believes about the origin of humans, one has to deal with significant essential differences between humans and animals.

Our idea of how we as humans relate to the world and universe around us begins with our interpretation of what we see. However, it is also informed by how we interpret the *motion* of the things we see. The ancients interpreted the world as animated by various gods. These gods were numerous, manipulative, and unpredictable; people therefore saw themselves as living, often in fear, in a mysterious and unpredictable world.

In medieval times, the triune God of Christianity was thought to move the world and determine history. The God of Christianity revealed himself through Christ and the scriptures as good, but God was also thought to be mysterious. The influence of Augustine (influenced himself by Plato) and paganism contributed to the idea that the word moved mysteriously. A certain amount of fear, both of the world and the God who controlled it, remained.

During the twelfth century people's relationship with the world began to change. Through the influence of Aristotle and the rise of the medieval university, thinkers progressed from the idea that God directly moved the world to the idea that God moved the world through the invisible world of essence—Aristotle's magical ontological watch. At the centre of the magical ontological watch was the triune God of Christianity. Thinkers began to link the motion of the ontological watch with the God who revealed his nature through Christ and the scriptures.

Rather than being fearful of the world and its motion, these thinkers began to see the world as an exciting place to discover. While the world was still viewed as magical and mysterious, Aristotle's assumption that the motion of things could be explained began to take hold. Because the triune God of Christianity was at the centre of the world of essence, learning about how things moved also enabled one to learn about the nature of God.

In this way Natural Philosophy and Theology were related. Both disciplines studied the nature of God. Theology revealed the nature of God through special revelation, while Natural Philosophy revealed the nature of God through the world's movement. By the age of the Enlightenment, people began to see the world and the planets moving with precise order and reliability. This order and reliability was transposed onto the God who created the world; the fearsome, mysterious God of the Medieval Era became the watchmaker God, a figure who set the world in motion but played no active part in its history or ongoing movement.

The Enlightenment thinkers saw themselves as mastering the fearsome and mysterious world of the Medieval Age. They were full of confidence in their own ability to explain apparent mysteries. Such was their zeal that anything which remained mysterious was shunned or explained away, including events in the life of Christ. Miracles were simply untenable for Enlightenment thinkers, even miracles confirmed by hundreds of witnesses.

The shift in thought during the Age of Enlightenment allowed science to break free of its prior hindrances, but in many ways the shift was like a bad romantic break-up with negative effects lasting to the present day. The assumptions that powered the rise of science were the fruit of a two millennia old tree rooted in Greek philosophy and Christianity. Enlightenment thinkers enjoyed the fruit of the tree, but they also wanted to chop it down. Their unquestioned faith in reason's power to explain everything transferred to all areas of knowledge, including theology, sociology, anthropology and ethics. The mystery of being human dulled.

As a result of the Renaissance and Enlightenment, humans began to conceive their relationship to the surrounding world differently. During the Renaissance, humans and the greater world took on more prominence in religious painting. Renaissance painters placed humans on more equal footing with God; they saw humans as beings taking ownership of their world. Through faith in reason's power to explain, Enlightenment man made many important discoveries, overcoming the fears and superstitions that marked the Medieval Age.

This same spirit carried through to philosophy, previously dominated by Aristotle. Rene Descartes (1596-1650), full of confidence after his success in reforming mathematics, sought to reinvent philosophy by freeing it from Aristotle and Metaphysics and proceeding from secure assumptions. But the only thing Descartes could ultimately be sure about was his own existence. Thus his tenet: *I think therefore I am*. Descartes was willing to assume that other objects had an independent existence outside his head, but almost all subsequent philosophers (except Locke, Hume, and Kant) were unwilling to make this assumption.

Indeed, by the twentieth-century, the reference point for philosophers became either words or reality as phenomena.

Philosophers were unwilling to assume that objects existed independently outside of their heads. I will say more about the study of reality as phenomena, or *Phenomenology*, shortly, but it is important to first address the assumption that words can be used as a reference point for reality.

Words only have meaning in the context of an assumed reality. Words function to describe reality, but they are not reality in and of themselves. In reading this book, it is ultimately what stands behind important words, like *good* and *justice*, that gives them their definition, not the words in and of themselves. Words like "if" and "or" may appear to be exceptions, but these words only have meaning in the context of an assumed reality or accompanying nouns and verbs. By themselves words are thus an insufficient basis of knowledge.

In twentieth-century philosophy, Phenomenology became the dominant view, held by philosophers like Sartre, Heidegger, and Husserl. However, its origins lie with Arthur Schopenhauer (1788-1860). Phenomenology, simply put, assumes that reality exists purely as phenomena outside of and within our heads. Schopenhauer believed in an outside world, but he also believed he could influence the world through the mind, leading to his tenet: *the world is my idea* (played out in the 1997 movie *Life is Beautiful*). Out of this view of reality, *Existentialism* emerged. Although Soren Kierkegaard (1813-1855) is known as the Father of Existentialism, its source is actually phenomenologists like Schopenhauer, Husserl (1859-1938), and particularly Sartre (1905-1980), one of the most influential twentieth-century philosophers.

Everyone in the West is influenced by Existentialism,

whether they know it or not. Existentialism focuses on the individual human consciousness and one's subjective experience of reality. The main tenet of Existentialism is the idea that how we feel as we go through life is ultimately more important than the consequences of our actions. Its result can be seen in almost any modern commercial, which focuses on communicating how someone will *feel* as a result of purchasing the product rather than on the practical consequences of buying the product.

Due to the influence of existentialism, views of contentment in the West center around how one feels moment by moment. They have less to do with overall feelings of happiness and satisfaction as a person examines his or her life. Western drug culture is a symptom of existentialism: conditions of the soul are often treated as chemical problems with an immediate chemical fix in the form of a pill or drug.

Existentialism, with its roots in Phenomenology, has also had important effects on how humans think about their *Telos* or purpose. Through Phenomenology, the idea that we are simply projections of our consciousness has filtered into mainstream culture. Individuals come to believe that by reading the right books, going to the right school, or thinking the right thoughts, irrespective of individual essence or cultural and family handicaps, they can be whoever they want.

Phenomenology assumes an outside reality, but that reality exists as phenomena rather than independently existing objects that move through time. While phenomenologists reject the assumption that objects have an independent existence outside our heads, they also reject *solipsism,* the idea that reality only exists in our heads.

While all modern philosophers have sought to reject the charge of solipsism (with varying degrees of success; Schopenhauer simply said a solipsist was like a madman in a block house) the line between solipsism and phenomenology is fine.

Phenomenologists have had to respond to solipsism because treating objects as phenomena does not guarantee they have an actual existence outside our heads. Phenomena out there may exist purely within our minds. Solipsism is a serious problem because it would result in the cessation of any university philosophy department—there is simply no point explaining a reality that only exists in one person's head. For this reason, phenomenologists, including Sartre, defend against solipsism and continue to assume that reality exists as phenomena outside of our heads.

The best way to understand Phenomenology is to think about a film. When we watch films, we are in fact watching a frame-by-frame advancement which gives the impression of ongoing action and narrative. Because no film has an infinite frame rate, it could be argued that the objects and people in a film cease to exist between frames. If we viewed films from a phenomenological perspective, we would agree that things appear on the screen, but we would have no basis to actually connect what we are seeing frame-by-frame with independently-existing objects. Although objects and people may look the same between frames, this is not guaranteed.

The only reason a film means anything to us is because we assume that what we see in each frame continues existing between frames. Similarly, reality only has meaning if we assume that things (including people) exist independently of our ability to perceive their ongoing existence. The challenge that confronts any version of phenomenology is thus explaining why reality means anything or is even worth explaining.

In many ways modern philosophy has gone full circle back to Parmenides. If reality only consists of what is sensed, there is no basis for the assumption that objects exist independent of our ability to sense them. Further, there is no basis for assuming that objects or people change through time. Parmenides came to exactly this conclusion two-and-a-half thousand years ago when he stated that motion—and thus reality—was impossible to explain and ultimately meaningless.

It is because phenomenologists do not assume the independent existence of objects that they face the problem of *temporality*: or explaining why moment-by-moment existence has any meaning. To address this problem, phenomenologists like Heidegger and Sartre needed a foundation of being upon which to ground their philosophy and give meaning to reality. For Heidegger the foundation of being, *Dasein* or *being there,* required a person to transcend oneself in order to be able to give meaning to reality. Through transcending individual consciousness, one was able to find meaning in the moment-by-moment existence of the world.

Sartre was uncomfortable with Heidegger's foundation of being because it diminished individual consciousness. For Heidegger, one had to step outside of oneself to comprehend reality. But transcending oneself for reality to mean anything also necessitated transcending one's individual consciousness. Sartre disliked Heidegger's view because it treated human consciousness as an ecstatic project beyond the individual human. Under Heidegger's philosophical system, it is very difficult for humans to have real and concrete relationships.

Sartre could not relegate human consciousness to an ecstatic project. Instead, he formulated his foundation of being as a dialectic *within* each human or object. For Sartre, each object had an individual essence, its *in-itself*, and this essence incarnated itself to resemble the object's appearance: its *for-itself*. The dialectic between each object's in-itself and for-itself anchored reality and gave things meaning. Sartre's dialectic was in fact borrowed from Hegel, who used the dialectical model to define the good in ethics. By anchoring the foundation of being within each human, as opposed to Heidegger's detached *Dasein*, Sartre was able to give individuals meaning and importance. Thus his book: *Existentialism is a Humanism*.

Although Sartre could be labeled a phenomenologist, his assumptions about reality actually came close to assuming the independent existence of objects. Objects existed in and for themselves and manifested themselves in their physical appearance; they had an independent existence and could move through time.

Although Sartre made concrete relationships possible, he had difficulty with universal causality. Sartre addresses causality in his writings, but he defines it very differently from the Enlightenment thinkers. In Sartre's philosophical system, things did not have a trajectory or potentiality as in Aristotle's system. Sartre believed each individual object's dialectic of the in-itself and for-itself caused it to move. In other words, motion could not be predicted because it was determined by each individual object's unique essence.

A good example is the phenomena of thirst. For Sartre, thirst does not originate from the causal operations of the human body but from the dialectic of consciousness within each human. Thirst manifested itself through the *in-itself* and ultimately completed itself through the *for-itself*—drinking a glass of water. For Sartre, thirst resulted not from universal causality but from a process within the dialectic consciousness of each individual human. A person could thus choose whether they needed to drink water to survive.

By redefining causality, Sartre also made each person a potential controller of his or her own world and movement. He thus abandoned universal causality. According to Sartre, a person who is anxious about contingency acts in bad faith. He or she has the potential to control reality and define causality. For Sartre, the potential of each person is not given but created through his or her own essence or dialectic of consciousness.

The idea that a human can control his or her own world may seem hard to believe, but Sartre's ideas about contingency are actually consistent with his assumptions about reality. In the same way, our assumptions about reality ultimately determine how we deal with contingency. Whether we believe pure reason, a foundation of being, or even our consciousness moves reality, we put our faith in this distinct entirety or understanding.

As humans, we all walk by faith in something or someone. Just as scientists walk by faith in universal causality, we walk by faith in that which will enable us to reach our idea of the contented life. In dealing with contingency or events beyond our control, we put our faith in the most powerful being that we can trust within our view of reality, whether that be ourselves, another person, or an invisible foundation of being standing behind reality.

When Frodo learns of The Ring's significance and his subsequent peril, he turns to the most powerful being he can trust, Gandalf, for help. Frodo particularly looks to Gandalf to provide an explanation as to how The Ring, the crux of Middle Earth's history, came to a hobbit of the Shire who was not even looking for it.

"It was not Gollum, Frodo, but the Ring itself that decided things," says Gandalf. "The Ring left him. It abandoned Gollum. Only to be picked up by the most unlikely person imaginable: Bilbo from the Shire!

"Behind that there was something else at work, beyond any design of the Ring-maker. I can put it no plainer than by saying that Bilbo was *meant* to find the Ring, and *not* by its maker. In which case you also were meant to have it. And that may be an encouraging thought."

Behind the events of Middle Earth there is indeed something at work. Frodo is immersed in the created reality of J.R.R. Tolkien, author of *The Lord of the Rings* and creator of Middle Earth. Although the creator and author of history on Middle Earth chooses to remain hidden and unseen, throughout the story Tolkien uses characters like Gandalf and Galadriel to encourage characters like Frodo, giving them hope that things will work out in the end.

Tolkien's world is not one of disinterested characters sleepwalking toward the after-life, but of characters who care about the course of their existence and thus about the events and history of Middle Earth. If Frodo's peaceful life takes a sudden turn for the worse upon learning the significance of The Ring, then through

Gandalf Tolkien ensures that Frodo has hope things will work out for him and Middle Earth.

Middle Earth's history is not viewed by characters like Frodo as a random set of events leading to a destination in which no one has an interest. Frodo desires a good end for his own life; he therefore has a vested interest in the fate of the Shire and Middle Earth—a fate now tied up with his own path as reluctant Ring bearer. Frodo's assumption of meaning and purpose in the course of his own life leads him to assume meaning and purpose in the greater history of Middle Earth.

Civilizations record history because they assume meaning and purpose in the events which make up their history. The Hebrews provide one of the oldest examples in their belief that Yahweh formed the nation of Israel and led his people to be a great nation. Likewise, the Greeks and Romans recorded history because they believed their gods led them to be a great civilization.

In the same way that philosophers attempt to explain reality because they believe such explanations are possible, people write history because they believe a purpose and direction is associated with it. Herodotus (484–425 BCE) is regarded as the first historian in the West and the father of Western history; he is believed to be the first person to gather materials, check sources, and write an organized history.

Herodotus' main work, *The Histories,* describes various conflicts in Greek history. Herodotus did not write *The Histories* because he had nothing better to do with his time; he wrote because he believed in an underlying meaning and purpose to Greek history, particularly in their conflicts and heroic deeds such as defending Greece from enemies like the Persians.

History writing is more than simply recording facts and events. It is about selecting the events and facts the historian considers most important. No objective historical sources exist because any source is *already* an interpretation by the author. The selection process is shaped by where the author sees history going and what the author considers the underlying meaning and purpose of that history to be. The job of the historian is to understand both the original author's and his or her own interpretation of history.

As Gandalf interprets the history of Middle Earth, he believes The Ring has a will of its own. But he also believes that "something else" is at work—this something else caused Frodo to get The Ring and is ultimately working toward the good of Middle Earth. The lore-masters kept records of Middle Earth's history. Gandalf knows that history because they all assume a meaning and purpose in which Frodo now plays a central part.

Through Gandalf, Tolkien steps into the history of Middle Earth. Gandalf causes Bilbo to go on his first adventure with the dwarves and guides him along the way; Gandalf comes to Frodo, warns him of his peril, and tells him to leave The Shire. At the battle of Minas Tirith, Gandalf brings hope to the besieged city and plays a central role in defending it.

But many of the Hobbits of the Shire are ignorant of the peril facing Middle Earth, the Shire, and they themselves. For them, the story of the Shire is the only story worth knowing; they take a dim view of Gandalf, who is known as a disturber of the peace. Most hobbits don't want anything to do with him.

Despite the ambivalence of the hobbits, Gandalf ultimately

rescues The Shire from destruction and effects the destruction of The Ring. Tolkien is the grand composer of the story of Middle Earth and its history, and through Gandalf he steps into his created world at critical points, bringing about the good end he has in mind for Middle Earth and the beings who dwell there. Characters like Frodo can legitimately hope for a good outcome because the overall *telos* of events on Middle Earth is toward the good.

# CHAPTER 10

## *The Bug goes East*

After three days in Tijuana Nate and I were ready to get back to the States. We packed our bags, ate breakfast, and hailed a taxi. A dusty yellow cab came to a halt in front of our hotel; soon we were back at the border going through US Customs. The Bug waited faithfully for us in the parking lot, with everything as we'd left it. To our surprise The Bug started first try—it was nice to return to the familiarity.

Our plan was to spend the day at the beach in San Diego, then make our way toward Las Vegas: "You'll love Vegas, man," Nate said. "You walk into these casinos, there's all this ringing and dinging from the slot machines, people all excited—and the food! Man, you pay $20 and you can eat as much as you want!"

As I think back, I realize I almost enjoyed hearing Nate talk about Vegas more than actually being in Vegas.

It was a glorious summer day in San Diego; we made a beeline for the beach. Within the hour we were driving along Mission Beach looking for a place to park. The beach in San Diego was just as I imagined it: white sand, breaking waves, lots of beach babes. We walked along, breathing in the fresh, salty air and looking for a place to pitch our towels. As I settled onto the sand, I realized that this trip with Nate was exactly what I'd needed—and an internship at a pipe factory in Pennsylvania was the *last* thing.

It was hard to reconcile my orderly and predictable student life at Penn State with all that had happened. Living with Nate meant an entirely different existence, even in the sleepy town of Mercer. Before this trip, stuff like getting chased out of Hooters or running across a bridge late at night in my underwear didn't happen in a few years, let alone a few days.

One could not travel with Nate for a summer and not be changed. Although Nate was a little overconfident at times, he didn't seem confined by the limitations I put on myself. Nate was adventurous, and he was fun to be with. Throughout the trip I heard many a bizarre story, some of which left me crying with laughter. I also loved hearing about Nate's zany life philosophies— his zest for life was contagious and I often wondered where he got his energy.

Not all Nate's wild desires played out during our trip, but in him I saw a different way of living. Why not do something crazy or outrageous? Why not think about boarding a cruise ship and having a blast in the Caribbean? Why not dream of doing great things in your lifetime?

The summer felt like a different existence, and I liked it. I had joined Nate's family for a month, lived with Tony for a month, and spent the rest of the time on the road. As I sat on the beach and looked out at the ocean, I felt myself beginning to emerge from my box.

In many ways I had built the box around myself, but I had also let expectations and social mores play a part in its construction. The box was my limited idea of who I thought I was combined with the collective ideas of who other people thought I should be. It stifled me, and it drove my desire for travel and escape.

Nate was one of the few characters I had met who didn't seem to know boxes like mine even existed. If Nate wanted to do something like swim across a river naked, he went ahead and did it. He wasn't labelled "Crazy Nate" for no reason. He didn't care about the complex social mores so prevalent at college. Nate was not oblivious; he just preferred to be who he was instead of participating in other peoples' social games.

Nate was very much a free spirit. In spending time with him, I began to like the idea of simply being who I was, free from other people's thoughts and ideas. Nate had large, crazy dreams and he went ahead and chased them. Uncle Synick wasn't a chick magnet or someone with social clout; Nate just liked hanging out with him and enjoyed his company—so he did. Nate was happy—"Crazy Nate" label or not.

Seeing how Nate lived gave me a new perspective on life. His approach probably cost him a few friends at Beaver Hall, but it was a small price to pay for the excitement and freedom he seemed to enjoy. I still had a long way to go in the process of actualization, but by spending the summer with Nate I began to see the joy and freedom to be found in being honest and true to myself.

"What time do you have, Brett?" Nate asked. We'd been napping on the beach for about an hour. I squinted at my watch.

"Um...it's around twelve-thirty."

"Okay," said Nate. Within a minute he'd drifted back to sleep.

Our existence was simple. There was nothing to worry about except sunburn or the odd wave washing too close to our towels.

Our plan for the evening was to sleep on the beach. I would sleep in The Bug; Nate wanted to sleep outside. After locating the ideal spot, we began our nightly ritual of finding cheap food and getting set up to rest. On this particular night, we decided to splash out and buy a hotdog for dinner, then take in more of the beach before dark. After sunset, we headed back to The Bug. I set up shop on the pile in the back seat while Nate unrolled his sleeping bag. Before long I was falling asleep to the sound of the ocean.

The next morning squawking sea gulls woke me. Nate was still sound asleep outside. I sat and watched the ocean until he woke up—I could have easily spent another day in San Diego. After about a half an hour, Nate began to show signs of life.

"How'd you sleep, Nate?"

"Wow, I wish I could sleep here every night. I love sleeping on the beach," he said, looking out at the ocean. "What's the time?"

"It's just after seven-thirty," I said.

"Long drive today. I guess we should get ready."

It was about six hundred miles from San Diego to the Grand Canyon. We were aiming for Williams (about 60 miles from the Grand Canyon) so we could see the canyon early the next morning and arrive in Vegas in the afternoon. If we got into Vegas just after lunch the next day, Nate reasoned, we would have a better chance of finding a good—and cheap—place to stay.

We packed up and ate some granola bars for breakfast. The Bug started without much trouble and before long we were on Highway 15 heading north. It was another hot day on the road, but we were excited by the prospect of seeing Las Vegas and the Grand Canyon. Nate had seen both before but this was my first time seeing either.

Nate had mentioned Vegas whenever we talked about going west. Now that the dream was becoming a reality, he talked about it even more. Vegas was a heavenly city for Nate. Something about the possibility of winning money—and even seeing other people win—was irresistible. The abundance of cash up for grabs, free drinks, skimpily-clad bar maids, cheap food and accommodation were all precious commodities in Nate's economy. Las Vegas seemed designed especially for him.

After a several hours on Highway 15, we turned and headed east on Highway 40. Before we made the turn we saw road signs for Las Vegas. Nate knew his dream was becoming a reality—soon he'd be in paradise. We were excited.

By lunch we'd reached the town of Kingman. Williams was about 100 miles away. The Bug, steady as ever, showed no signs of being affected by the heat. Things were a bit toasty inside, but we were consoled by the prospect of an air-conditioned hotel room in Williams. The transition from the beach to arid desert was nonetheless a stark contrast.

We arrived in Williams mid-afternoon, and for the latter part of the day we lay on our beds watching the Olympics on television. The Olympics had started a few days earlier, on July 19$^{th}$. It was somewhat ironic that although we had gone to Atlanta because of the Olympics, our first look at the games was via a small television in a hotel room in Williams, Arizona. I turned up the air-conditioning and watched track events on the tiny set in the corner of our room while Nate snoozed.

The next day was as hot as the previous one, so we were keen to hit the road early.

"It's going to be a roaster, man," Nate said, winding down his window. We arrived at the Grand Canyon mid-morning and gingerly got out of The Bug.

To stand on one side and look into the canyon was like looking at another planet. The other wall seemed an eternity away. The red earth and the towering walls set the Grand Canyon apart from anything I had ever seen. It was hard for me to believe one river could account for this vast gorge in the middle of the desert.

Even after millions of years.

Our initial plan had been to look at the canyon and then head off to Vegas. But when we arrived we saw that some people were going to hike down into the canyon and stay at a hostel at the bottom called The Phantom Lodge. We expected the hostel to be completely booked up, but to our surprise there were vacancies.

"I know we wanted to get to Vegas today, but I think this could be cool," Nate said. "You up for a hike, Brett?"

"Yeah; if there are vacancies we should definitely do it."

I loved the way our adventure just unfolded. Most people hiking down the canyon had been planning for months if not years—but Nate and I spent all of ten minutes working out the hike down.

The temperature in the canyon that day was 116 °F (which may have accounted for the vacancies in the hostel), and we were instructed by the park ranger to carry at least two gallons of water. We acquired some, donned the enormous sombreros we had picked up at the Atlanta flea market, and began our descent into the enormous gorge.

I felt small. All of a sudden my world and the cares of my life seemed insignificant. The canyon had a way of swallowing up my worries. The sweltering heat, however, caused new worries for other hikers. Even early in the day we encountered people struggling in the heat; one woman had to be transported away by medics because of heat exhaustion. Periodically a mule team would pass us on the trail down. It was remarkable how surefooted the mules were on the rocky trail despite the weight they carried.

We had thought two gallons of water was an outrageous amount, but we soon began to see the ranger's wisdom. As we descended into the searing canyon, we caught sight of the Colorado River. The green water was a heavenly sight, and we quickened our pace. We crossed the bridge over the river and headed for a natural pool to cool off.

We had heard the water was cold, but until we stepped in we didn't understand. The water was *so* cold that it was painful and difficult to stay in for more than thirty seconds. The air temperature was 116 °F, yet the water below was just above 32°F — the pool had not long ago been glacier ice somewhere in the Rocky Mountains.

Nate and I beached ourselves and regulated our body temperature by getting in and out of the pool. The temperature difference between the air and the water was so great, however, that it soon became uncomfortable. We weren't far from the hostel; we decided to check in and return later.

Along the path to the hostel, we approached an unusually large group of people near the riverbank. On closer investigation we realized the group was surrounding a medical crew trying to resuscitate a boy who had collapsed. The chipper holiday spirit of the hikers in the canyon evaporated as a glorious day taking in the sights turned into a battle for the boy's life. The medical team kept trying to reassure the onlookers and keep them calm, but the boy was turning an unhealthy blue. Some bystanders frantically gathered water and poured it over the boy. We waited, unable to do more than watch.

Earlier in the day we'd seen this boy, with a group of older people, going down into the canyon. As his group neared the bottom, we learned, the boy got excited about swimming in the river and ran ahead. The next time they saw him he was lying unconscious, surrounded by medical personnel. He was originally found on the path leading to the river; the medics moved him closer to the river to cool down his body. The backdrop of the fast-moving river and the vast canyon combined to make the situation even more dramatic.

It was hard to believe the lifeless body in front of us was the same energetic boy. A chopper came and airlifted him out. The group slowly disbanded. We didn't know for sure that he had died, but the consensus among us was that there was little hope.

After riding an emotional roller coaster, we had no choice but to follow the crowd to The Phantom Ranch. We were a diverse group, but a solidarity had developed after hiking the canyon and seeing the fallen boy. We had all seen great and tragic things that day.

Once checked in, Nate and I decided to go back to the pool.

"So, you think that kid is going to live?" I asked Nate.

"Sure, he'll make it; he'll be airlifted to a hospital where they have equipment and doctors...you know."

It was hard for me to understand Nate's optimism. I didn't know much about medicine, but I knew a person who wasn't breathing and had no heartbeat couldn't live long. I didn't know if Nate was holding onto false hope or if he really believed the boy would live.

The boy died, likely from heat exhaustion. I don't know exactly when, but in seeing him lying by the river, surrounded by medics and volunteers, I saw a dead body for the first time. Even while I hoped the boy would live, I was in a slight state of shock. He was so young. I think Nate and I both learned from that experience that death was close to everyone, young and old alike.

We remained silent as we walked past the vacant spot where the boy had been treated. At the pool we took in more of our impressive surroundings, then after a few hours we went back to the hostel and prepared dinner—a can of baked beans or soup. The sun slowly descended; darkness took over the canyon. The only light emanated from our hostel, a tiny speck within the vast gorge.

When darkness gave way to the rising sun, however, the hostel became a hive of activity. The hike out of the canyon was estimated at 4-5 hours and starting early meant avoiding the hottest part of the day. Nate and I packed our gear, filled our water bottles, and put on our sombreros. I started the ascent strong, but after the halfway point I had to rest and cool off every fifteen minutes. Nate powered up the canyon— a truly remarkable feat. I had assumed we were at roughly the same fitness level, but Nate left me in the dust.

Although it was a challenging climb, a cheerful attitude prevailed among the ascending pilgrims; with every step we came closer to our objective. A sense of community sprang up: we were sharing an amazing experience, and we were keenly aware of the perils of hiking in such extreme heat. At various times we redistributed water to ascending and descending parties who needed more, supporting and encouraging each other.

Nate stopped and talked to other pilgrims periodically, enabling me to catch up; occasionally, I got to join some of the conversations. We neared the top and everyone grew excited as the final goal became visible. It was rewarding to see how far we had come—looking down at the vast canyon below, it seemed like we had just scaled a large mountain. After taking photos and saying goodbyes, it was time to continue our journey.

A possible reason for Nate' quick ascent was his eagerness to reach Las Vegas. After we pitched our packs and sombreros into The Bug, we headed west. Nate noticed the first road sign directing us towards Las Vegas.

"Vegas baby, here we come!" Nate yelled.

Heaven for Nate was about three hours away and nothing was going to stop him. His excitement was contagious. We entered the hallowed city and pulled up at a small, non-descript hotel on the strip.

"Yeah, this looks really cheap; look, Brett, twenty dollars a night!"

We parked and checked in. About two minutes after we had placed our belongings in the room, Nate was ready.

"Well, Brett, I'll see you out there. All the casinos are that way," Nate said, pointing briefly as he walked out the door. I had no hope of catching up with Nate so I rested for a while in the room and then went out to look around. I don't remember much about my first night in Vegas other than piles of raunchy fliers lying around and lots of people.

The next morning we discussed the upcoming day.

"We should go swimming at the MGM casino," Nate said.

"Don't you need to be a guest to use the pool?"

"Nah, man, you can just walk on through; tell the security

person you're a guest and make up a room number if they ask."

Security at Las Vegas casinos has certainly improved since the likes of Nate and me were there, but that day Nate's plan worked perfectly. Before we knew it we were sitting by the pool at MGM absorbing sun rays.

The pool was a massive upgrade from the 20-foot backyard pond at our hotel. The pool at MGM was like an oasis. Nate and I found some empty chairs and took in the scene. From where we sat, the pool seemed to have no dimensions. Multitudes of like-minded vacationers collectively basked in the sunshine and sipped pina coladas; sounds of rushing water and shrill voices drifted toward us. The pool was a giant aquatic playground filled with children tossing balls, families playing, and people like Nate and I taking it all in. The day before Nate and I had been sweating our way out of the Grand Canyon. Now we were sitting at a heavenly paradise.

We spent the day swimming and sunbathing. Finally, our stomachs began to direct our thoughts away from the pool.

"Man, I'm hungry," Nate shouted. We were relaxing in one of the whirlpools.

"You got any ideas?" I said, moving closer so I could hear him.

"Well, I've heard the buffet at Treasure Island is good; it costs $20 but it's all-you-can-eat."

"Works for me," I said. "Let's dry off and go."

From poolside MGM we simply slipped our shirts and sandals on and walked over to Treasure Island. Nate and I probably violated the dress code, but so many people were going in and out that no one tried to stop us.

The buffet at Treasure Island was a stunning abundance of the best food I had ever seen. Overflowing baskets of bread, massive bowls filled with shrimp, elaborate salads, steaming soups—it felt like we were in a medieval king's court. Compared to our usual canned soup and baked beans, the options were almost impossible to comprehend.

"Wow, I wish they had something like this at Penn State," I said, making headway on my second plate of shrimp.

"I'm sure the football players would say the same thing. Those guys are always chowing down in the cafeteria," Nate said.

After five or six platefuls of food we began to feel the limitations of our stomachs and finished up with dessert. If we had any vitamin deficiencies, this meal addressed them. We slowly made our way back to the hotel and let our stomachs go to work.

After a few days of relaxing in Vegas, Nate returned from his wanderings with a dejected look on his face.

"Okay, man, I'm out of money; time to go home."

Nate had hoped to win big and stay for a long time, but that wasn't happening. The only thing to do now was go home. It was sad to think our adventure was coming to an end, but I suppose we did have to make our way back at some point.

A little more than two months had passed since we left Mercer, but school didn't start at Penn State for another five weeks. Nate's desire for adventure was truly remarkable; he wanted to do a Caribbean cruise and travel through South America. If there was any kind of fun to be had, anywhere in the world, Nate was up for it. But all these options required at least some money, and now Nate was battling to pay his share of the gas to get us home.

We spent our last evening in Las Vegas preparing for the journey home. It was an abrupt end to our adventure but such was the nature of our trip. We checked out of the hotel and loaded the car. After a half hour, we reached the nervous moment when we attempted to start The Bug. After some prolonged wire shaking, the long journey home began.

We motored north. Before long we were driving through Wyoming, heading east on I-90 toward Ohio. The mood in The Bug was different now; fun and adventure had turned into making our way home. It was also cooler now that we were further north, so we planned to drive during the day and rest at night.

The Bug had performed admirably on our trip but unfortunately it wasn't able to grow its own rubber. The tires were getting to a point where you could actually see the metal reinforcement. Somewhere in South Dakota, Nate took a corner too fast. It didn't help our cause that it was raining, but Nate was driving way above the speed limit. Before we knew it, we found ourselves off the side of the highway facing oncoming traffic.

# CHAPTER 11

## *The Hope of Redemption*

On September 22$^{nd}$, 2004, three hundred and twenty-four people boarded Flight Oceanic 815 in Sydney, Australia. The purposes of those boarding were as varied as the passengers, but they all expected to land fourteen hours later in Los Angeles and continue their life journey. They anticipated a long, uneventful flight that would fade from their memories as soon as they landed.

But Oceanic 815 never made it to Los Angeles. Fourteen hours after take off, the survivors found themselves sitting around signal fires on a tropical island beach. Instead of passing through customs and getting their luggage, they huddled under temporary shelters to stay dry. For the seventy-two survivors, a routine flight turned into a daily battle for survival on The Island.

The crash of Oceanic 815 marked the beginning of a long journey on The Island for seven of the survivors. Jack, Kate, Jin, Sun, Sayid, Hurley, and Sawyer, strangers when they boarded, eventually formed a virtual family. In the last season of *Lost*, six of the seven became candidates to replace Jacob, a mysterious figure who invites and brings people to The Island.

Immediately after the crash, the Losties expect rescue within a day or two. But as the weeks turn into months, they begin to make the painful realization that they might never see home again. The Island becomes their permanent reality; the people and things that characterized their normal life back home are reduced to fading hopes.

For some of the Losties, the transition to life on The Island is less painful than others. Locke is happy to leave the wreckage of his old life behind and begin anew. Rose, who expected to die within the year from cancer, is miraculously healed by The Island. Sun and Jin sought to escape Sun's domineering father, who was creating trouble in their marriage; The Island turned out to be the only place on Earth where he couldn't reach them.

Although all the Losties (except Locke) want to leave The Island, the crash and resulting experiences provide them with an unexpected opportunity to reflect upon the course of their lives.

*The Hope of Redemption*

The Island has a strange way of unlocking their past, particularly those incidents that the Losties want to sweep under the rug.

When Kate Austen boarded Oceanic 815, she was accompanied by US Air Marshal Edward Mars. Kate, on the run after murdering her stepfather, Wayne, was wanted for other crimes including her involvement in another man's death. Kate fled to Australia to escape, but the long arm of the law caught up with her. Flying back to the United States in handcuffs, Kate knew she faced a long jail sentence.

But Kate's life was about to take a dramatic turn. After miraculously surviving the plane crash, Kate found herself a free woman. She gets rid of her handcuffs as the plane goes down; in the crash, the air marshal is seriously injured. No one on The Island knows about her past except the marshal, who is unlikely to survive his injuries.

Kate thus believes she might finally be free of her past, but before long Jack finds her mug shot in the marshal's jacket. He keeps his suspicions about Kate to himself until Hurley stumbles upon the mug shot in the medical tent.

"What's this? Uh, dude? Uh ... What do you think she did?"

"It's none of my business."

"She looks pretty hardcore," says a slightly disturbed Hurley.

"Hurley..." Jack says, and moves on to something else, avoiding the question.

Later that day, Hurley, still concerned, asks Jack if he spoke to Kate.

"So what'd she say?

"She didn't say anything."

"But you told her you knew?"

"I don't know anything."

"Well, you kind of know she's in that mug shot. And that we found those handcuffs. And that guy keeps mumbling, 'She's dangerous, she's dangerous' over and over."

"It's not my business. Not my problem," says Jack.

As Jack gets to know Kate, his attitude about her past changes. They fast become friends, but Kate's unresolved past inhibits their relationship.

As humans we all have a past, a record of our collective experiences in life. This past begins with the context into which we are born. Our context consists of multiple stories, including that of family and culture, and it is in this context that we begin the process of *actualization* described in Chapter Nine. Our context allows us to actualize by revealing who we are relative to the people and culture around us.

Unfortunately, as humans our context is never perfect. Tragically, many people's context resembles that of a nightmare. As long as our context consists of other people, it will always be imperfect because no human is ever fully actualized. In some cases the people who play important roles in our context are only at an elementary level of actualization themselves.

To acknowledge the imperfect nature of our past means that, as humans, we must have an idea or *reference point* for a perfect context. We may not be able to define that reference point, but we can know that imperfections exist in our context and ultimately the world due to our feelings and emotions.

# The Hope of Redemption

The reason we experience sadness and grief is because the world is not as it should be. In the same way that our context or past is marred by imperfections, the physical planet is also marred by imperfections such as earthquakes and other natural disasters. Misconceived ideas about how the world should work can result in premature sadness and grief, but it is generally accepted that natural disasters, murder, rape, torture, and cruelty are things that should not happen.

To be human, then, is to participate in an imperfect world. The idea that such imperfection can be healed or resolved brings us to the topic of this chapter: *Redemption*. Redemption comes from the Greek verb λυτρόω, which means to redeem or liberate by a ransom; in Greek culture it was typically used in regard to slaves who were redeemed or set free for a certain price.

But the idea of Redemption goes back further than the Greeks. The concept also appears in the Hebrew Scriptures in relation to Israel. In Jewish thought, Redemption is more than just redeeming slaves. It also applies to healing or fixing the world at large through the supernatural work of God. To this day, Jews believe that Yahweh will bring Redemption to Israel and carry out God's promises to Israel, his chosen nation.

In Christian thought, God redeems the world through its savior: Jesus Christ. According to the scriptures, Christ came into the world to bring supernatural Redemption. The vehicle of this Redemption continues in the form of the Church. The hope of Redemption exists for Christians because of their belief in a supernatural God who is able to make all things perfect through Christ, the redeemer and head of the Church.

Redemption is an important theme in the story of *Lost*. Locke and Rose are both supernaturally healed by The Island, and many of the Losties confront and deal with unresolved issues in their pasts. The Island brings change for the Losties who survive and many become convinced that they were meant to crash there.

Redemption is a powerful idea because it is through hope in Redemption that a person believes his or her situation in life can improve. In the case of ancient Greek slavery, Redemption meant hope that one day a slave could be free to live his or her own life. While slaves could escape by their own wits (as often happened in Greek and Roman times), many situations in life prevent a person from bringing about the life for which he or she hopes.

In many instances, The Hebrews found themselves unable to bring about the life for which they hoped. In the book of Genesis, Yahweh promised Abraham (18th-17th century BCE), who was living in the city of Ur (Southern Mesopotamia), that he and his descendants would become a great nation. But several hundred years later, the Hebrews found themselves enslaved in Egypt. While under the yoke of slavery, the Hebrews hoped for Redemption. Their hope was only realized through the guidance and supernatural power of Yahweh. Under the leadership of Moses, the Hebrews were freed from slavery in Egypt and entered the promised land.

But the Hebrews' hope of Redemption went beyond Israel becoming a great nation. The Hebrews believed the Messiah, who would be born in Israel, would ultimately redeem the world at large and bring about a new world order. Yahweh would thus bring about the perfection of his created world and of the nation he chose to bless all others.

As we look at the world today, it is obvious that we are a long way from perfection—natural disasters, wars, and genocide characterize our existence on Earth. The paradox of our world, however, is that although many imperfections exist, so too does mind-blowing order and perfection. The motion of the planets and stars has fascinated humans, especially the Babylonian astronomers, since time began. The intricacy and perfection of the human body has been an object of study as far back as Ancient Egypt and the Greek physician Hippocrates (sixth century BCE). The paradox of our world is that extravagant perfection and heartbreaking imperfection co-exist.

The order and perfection seen in the world's motion became the focus of 18th-century Enlightenment thinkers who believed the world was moved by a mechanical ontological watch. However, this view of the world did not fully explain the motion of human beings or the imperfections in the world. The ontological mechanical watch enabled many important discoveries during the Age of Reason, but wholesale use of pure reason to explain the world's motion, including that of human beings, ultimately came up short in explaining reality.

In his thought about the workings of the world, Aristotle assumed the good was the end to which all things aimed. Aristotle did not specifically define the good, but his reference point was the destination (or *telos*) to which all things actually moved in nature. Aristotle did not deal with imperfections within the physical world, such as earthquakes and disease, but he did have to deal with imperfections in regard to human motion.

At the beginning of the *Nicomachean Ethics*, Aristotle assumes all human action and inquiry moves toward the good. But he knew that within any Greek city imperfections or apparently evil actions such as murder and stealing persisted. In admitting that some actions were indeed wrong or evil, Aristotle assumed a form of the good separate from the visible world even though he rejected Plato's idea that the form of the good was separate from what happened in reality. Aristotle's reference point for the good was the content Greek city, but somehow he knew that the citizens of the perfectly content Greek city did not commit evil acts such as stealing or murder.

Humans have confronted the problem of *evil* since the beginning of time. In early Greek thought, evil came from Pandora's box. In Hebrew and Christian thought, evil entered the world when Adam and Eve ate fruit from the Tree of the Knowledge of Good and Evil. While cultural Metanarratives provide many explanations for the problem of evil, all attempts to explain its existence assume a reference point for the good, just as Aristotle did. Without a reference point for the good, evil simply ceases to exist.

More than two millennia after Aristotle, Frederick Nietzsche (1844-1900) argued in *Beyond Good and Evil* that Socrates invented the notion of the good. The problem with Nietzsche's argument is that all cultures before Socrates also believed in right and wrong ways of acting—and thus had an idea of the good. Socrates did not invent the idea of the good. Rather, he was troubled by the usage of the term to describe conflicting modes of action in Greek classics such as *The Odyssey* and *The Iliad*.

While Aristotle was unwilling to define the ultimate good,

he knew that when humans picked tangible objects as their ultimate good they were somehow *corrupted*. According to Aristotle, humans did apparently evil things when their passions led them to misconstrued ideas of the ultimate good. By encouraging the pursuit of virtues such as temperance, Aristotle sought to direct Greek citizens away from the objects of their passions and toward the golden mean.

Corruption is the state of a person being adrift from the person he or she is meant to be. Corruption is not the state of a child coming into maturity, but the state of a person no longer actualizing as an individual and therefore disconnected from his or her essence. Actualization is a life-long process, but it can be hindered or even halted through the corruption caused by the detrimental influence of unresolved past events.

As we grow and mature, we develop expectations about how we should be treated by family and friends. When we are growing up, the bulk of this expectation falls on our parents. To varying degrees they do or do not meet our expectations. As children we often don't know what is best for us, so the fact that our parents disappoint is not always bad. But when the treatment we receive continually disappoints us, especially treatment by those to whom we are close and who have responsibility over us, a debt begins to accumulate.

Soon after Kate kills her stepfather, she attempts to flee Iowa. The US Marshal Edward Mars arrests her.

"It's a long drive back to the arraignment; you comfy? Why now?" says Edward.

"What?" Kate asks.

"Nice, cornfed farm girl like yourself—no history of violence, straight A's, no record, couple of speeding tickets—just got to wonder, why'd you kill him now? Oh, right, yeah, don't tell me. You wouldn't want to incriminate yourself, not after you were so smart planning it. That jury back in Iowa sure ain't going to get hung up on pre-meditation. And a gas leak, come on, it's amateur hour from top to bottom."

"Sounds like you've got it all figured out."

"I do have you all figured out. White-trash mom divorces dad, starts up with some guy who's a drinker. He knocks her around a little bit, she marries him, because, you know, that's what happens. And then this drunk, this Wayne, he moves into your house, and you get to lay there every night and listen to him doing your mom right there in daddy's old bedroom. And even that wouldn't be so bad if he didn't beat her up all the time. But she loves him. She defends him. If that don't make a person want to kill somebody I don't know what does. But the question is now, why now? Why after all these years did you just decide to blow poor Wayne up? He come knocking on your door late at night?"

"He never touched me," says Kate.

For Kate, growing up with a stepfather like Wayne meant an enormous perssonal cost. Wayne, corrupted by alcoholism and other life choices, could not be a source of love, encouragement, and affirmation for Kate. Instead, he was a source of abuse and discouragement. The cost Kate had to bear in regard to Wayne led to her being handicapped in her development as a woman. This in turn affected her relationships with men, including Jack.

In her early years, Kate chose to endure Wayne, but when

she was twenty-four something caused her to snap. While making a birthday scrapbook for her supposed father, the honorable Sergeant Sam Austen, Kate realized he was in Korea up to four months before she was born. Kate came to the painful realization that Wayne was in fact her real father. Kate was able to cope with Wayne's failings if he was just a low-life stepfather, but when she found out the truth her hatred and resentment approached boiling point.

For Kate, nothing in the natural world could compensate for the personal cost of Wayne's failings, which affected Kate from the age of five into adulthood. Wayne's enormous debt against Kate multiplied when she found out that he was her real father, and Kate resolved to get rid of him.

Immediately after blowing up Wayne, Kate visits her mother, Diane, at the diner where Diane works.

"Coffee, pie, both?" Diane offers.

"How about a beer?"

"I'd like to see some I.D."

"I'm 24, Ma."

"You want to ride around on that deathtrap (motorcycle) of yours without a helmet—I'm not going to help your cause by getting you drunk."

"How's that wrist?"

"What, this? No, that shelf in the kitchen sticks out sometimes. You'd think I'd remember it was there, but I banged it."

"Don't," says Kate.

"I made my bed, Katherine."

"Well, your bed's gone, Ma."

"What?"

"What is this?"

"An insurance policy for the house."

"What? I never..."

"I took it out in your name."

"What did you do? Does Wayne know about this?"

"Just remember that you were here and you didn't see me, okay?"

"Katherine! What did you do?"

"I took care of you, Ma. I've got to go and you're not going to see me for awhile." Kate says. She leaves.

For most of her life Kate sought to break free of her past by running away. But even after Wayne's death, she was still not free of him. The memories of his abuse and failings lived on in Kate's memory—even on The Island, Kate cannot escape her past. The only way to be free is to let go of her resentment and hatred and forgive Wayne.

To forgive is to let go of harm done to us by other people. In Koine Greek the verb forgive, ἀπολύω, is the same word used to describe physically letting go of something or setting someone free. Forgiveness is also used in the world of banking when a bank forgives or lets go of debt against the bank.

But as humans it is not natural for us to forgive. Our natural response is instead to get even and take back what we believe has been stolen from us. If it is impossible for us to get back what has been taken, we still hold those responsible for our loss accountable. But in doing so we build up hatred and resentment toward our debtors. Kate cannot get back what has been taken from her; consequently she builds up hatred and resentment toward Wayne.

In the natural world forgiveness is difficult. For Kate to truly forgive Wayne, she must let go of his debt and be able to treat him as if the damage he caused never happened. While banks do forgive debts, it is rarely genuine forgiveness: it is unlikely the bank will treat the customer as if the debt never existed. In the natural world genuine forgiveness is in fact impossible—it is a supernatural act.

Diane was well aware of the enormous cost exacted upon her by Wayne. Diane suffered Wayne for years and bore the cost of his corruption. But rather than hating or resenting Wayne, Diane bore the cost with the wounds of her own body. While Kate built up resentment toward Wayne, Diane was able to genuinely forgive and continue to love him.

The miracle of love is that people can remain in close relationships with others despite their shortcomings. Even though Wayne exacted an enormous cost on Diane, she was able to forgive him and overlook his failings. With supernatural forgiveness, Diane was able to love Wayne through being able to truly forgive him his debts.

Ultimately, it is only supernatural forgiveness which can break the cycle of hatred and revenge. But the only way we can truly forgive others is if we have been truly forgiven ourselves. As humans, we cannot give what we have not received. This is especially true in regards to forgiveness. To forgive is to give a person underserved grace; we can only give undeserved grace if we have received it ourselves.

Being on The Island leads Kate to confront the past from

which she has been running. While helping Sawyer recover from a gunshot wound, the barely-conscious Sawyer suddenly grabs Kate and asks why she killed him. Kate believes Wayne himself is asking her this question. Traumatized, she runs into the jungle and attempts to come to terms with her actions. There, Kate encounters Jack.

"Kate, what the hell are you doing out here? What happened in the hatch, Kate? Why'd you leave? I come back—I find Sawyer just lying on the ground. You just took off..."

"Is he okay?"

"Yes, Kate, he's fine."

"I'm sorry."

"Are you?"

"Yeah, I'm sorry. I'm sorry that I am not as perfect as you. I'm sorry that I'm not as good."

"Okay, what's going on with you?"

"Just forget it."

On Oceanic 815, heading towards LA, Kate believed she was innocent. But when she confronts Jack in the jungle, Kate realizes she is ashamed of who she has become. Kate has feelings for Jack, but in being with him, she is no longer able to justify the bad things she has done or remain comfortable with the person she has become. In Jack, Kate sees the good person she wants to be. In Sawyer, she sees the corruption so engrained in herself that she is attracted to it.

After her encounter with Jack, Kate goes back to the hatch to confront Wayne.

"Can you hear me? Sawyer? Wayne? I'm probably crazy

and this doesn't matter, but maybe you're in there somehow. But you asked me a question. You asked me why I—why I did it. It wasn't because you drove my father away, or the way you looked at me, or because you beat her. It's because I hated that you were a part of me—that I would never be good. That I would never have anything good. And every time that I look at Sawyer—every time I feel something for him—I see you, Wayne. It makes me sick."

In making Wayne the object of her hatred, Kate becomes like the man she hates. In the same way, Sawyer becomes like the con man who destroyed his family. When Kate realizes Wayne is her real father, she also realizes that the corruption she saw in Wayne is also within her. But the corruption in Wayne was not given to Kate at birth. Rather, it grew out of Kate's hatred and resentment. Ultimately, part of Kate's motivation in killing Wayne was avenging what he had done to her. She couldn't see that her hatred of Wayne caused her to become like him.

When Kate finds out that Wayne is her real father, she gives up hope of being or having anything good. As long as Kate thought her real father was the honorable Sam Austin, she clung to that hope. But Kate's hope vaporized when she learned the truth. Kate realized she was a product of the very corruption she hated.

In her attraction to Jack, Kate begins to hope anew for good. The Island gives her a fresh start, and in spite of her unresolved past she begins to believe she can have good things in life. Although Kate is corrupted and disconnected from her essence, that essence still allows her to recognize the potential in Jack and in herself.

The hope of Redemption exists because our past does not

define us in the same way that our essence does. Corruption from an unresolved past can inhibit or block the actualization process, but it does not erase our constant essential core. We always have hope but inner corruption can only be reversed if we are genuinely able to forgive those who have hurt or disappointed us.

After a few days on The Island, the air marshal dies. Kate soon finds out that Jack knows about her mug shot.

"I want to tell you what I did—why he was after me."

"I don't want to know. It doesn't matter, Kate, who we were—what we did before this, before the crash. It doesn't really—three days ago we all died. We should all be able to start over," says Jack, looking out at the ocean.

After the crash there is a general belief among the Losties that everyone has received a new lease on life. The Island is seen as a way of re-setting past events and beginning anew. But the only way this can truly take place is if the Losties free themselves from their unresolved pasts. Being on The Island awakens the hope of Redemption in Kate, but the only way she can begin again is to deal with her reservoir of guilt and hatred.

For Kate, there is much to forgive—and even more of which she must be forgiven. Yet, it is difficult for Kate to be free of her past because the consequences of her actions cannot be simply reversed. Kate cannot bring Wayne back from the grave or revive the other man she killed. The only way Kate can be free of her guilt is to receive supernatural forgiveness which will in turn enable her to forgive.

Over the years, Kate's hatred and resentment accumulated like dry underbrush, needing only a small spark to ignite into an inferno. Finding out Wayne is her real father is the spark, but hatred does not fully explain Kate's actions. An obvious solution to her hatred and resentment is to leave home and forget. If Kate killed Wayne out of pure anger, she would have been satisfied by the deed itself. Instead, Kate carefully planned the killing to make it look like an accident and took out an insurance policy on the house to help her mother financially.

For much of her life, Kate had barely a mark against her name. She went to Sunday school, earned straight A's, and had no criminal record. Her only bad deed is stealing a New Kids on the Block lunchbox at the age of five. As she is about to leave the store, the owner grabs Kate and opens her bag.

"Mhm. Where'd you get this?"

"I got it over there," says Kate, pointing.

"I know you. You're Diane Austen's girl...what's your name?"

"Katie."

"Well Katie, I'm calling your mom, then the cops, because I don't tolerate stealing here, you understand?"

"No need to do that. I'll pay for it. I hope this is enough," says another man in the store. He gestures with several bills.

"Well, as long as somebody pays for it, I guess there's no harm done. But I don't want to see you in here ever again without your parents, you understand me?" The owner says to Kate.

"Thanks, mister," Kate says to the man.

"You're welcome," says the man, kneeling down to be at eye level with her. "You're not going to steal anymore, are you?"

Kate shakes her head no.

"Be good, Katie," the man says, and leaves.

In the last season of *Lost* The Island is revealed to be an opportunity for its inhabitants to overcome the flaws and the corruption that inhibit them. The man who paid for the stolen lunch box is none other than Jacob, the mysterious figure who brings people to The Island. As overseer of the candidates to replace him, Jacob has the ability to guide and direct all six, including Kate.

But, again, while flying to LA in handcuffs Kate believed she had been good throughout her life. Even though she was wanted for murder and other crimes, she believed her actions were justified. The problem for Kate is that Jacob defines what it means to be good—not her.

As humans, we all have an idea of the good. We don't wait for philosophers or categorical imperatives; out of necessity, we are forced to make hundreds of ethical choices every day of our lives. Over time we slowly build up an idea of what constitutes good or right action; this idea is what we endeavor to fulfill throughout our lives.

Our innate sense of the good stems from our inner essence, or *conscience,* and by this innate sense we can "just know" something is right or wrong without knowing why. In the same way that we interpret our essence and actualize, we also interpret our innate sense of the good and build up our idea of what such good entails.

It is because we interpret and build up our idea of the good that we can form incorrect or misguided ideas about what is good. Interpreting and building up our idea of the good is actually a complex process. Our ideas are influenced by our context; they are also influenced, and potentially corrupted, by our past, particularly those events most at odds with our inner essence. But the most important influence on our idea of the good is what we believe the *ultimate good* or *source of the good* to be.

As humans we tend to act in a way that preserves or helps us obtain this *ultimate good*. Although our lives consist of many good things, we do not view them all as equally good. As humans we *prioritize*; subsequently we decide on the ultimate good which all other goods serve. Because of this prioritizing, our idea of the good is not just a long list of rules. Rather, it is more like a flow chart aimed at preserving or obtaining our idea of the ultimate good.

I mentioned in Chapter Nine that, as a house is built with an ultimate good in mind, so our lives are built. Whatever our idea of the ultimate good, it forms the underlying motive behind all our actions. Our idea of the ultimate good may not be a definition of the ultimate good itself but an idea of what a good or *contented life* looks like, and this usually consists of various good things.

As Kate grew up and matured, she developed an idea of the contented life. Kate had a boyfriend, Tom; they hoped to marry and have many children. Kate wasn't as keen as Tom to settle down, but she knew that at some point she wanted that life. Even while Kate is on the run, she gravitates toward her idea of the contented life, marrying a policeman and building a household with him. When Kate leaves The Island in Season Five of *Lost,* she also gravitates toward her idea of the contented life, moving in with Jack and claiming Aaron as her son.

But Kate's idea of the contented life is about more than her own well-being. It includes the contentment of her mother. More than willing to leave home herself and be free of Wayne, Kate knew her mother would choose to remain and endure Wayne's abuse. As long as Wayne remained alive, Kate knew that her mother would never be free.

Though Kate thought killing Wayne would help her mother, it ultimately turns Diane against her. Soon after Kate is caught by Mars, a mysterious black horse causes their car to crash. Kate escapes. Discovering that her mother reported her to the authorities, Kate resolves to find out why Diane sided with the abusive Wayne. At great risk to herself, Kate meets her mother in the restroom of the diner where Diane works.

"Hi Mom."

"What are you doing here, Katherine?"

"You look good."

"I asked you what you are doing here."

"I wanna know why you told them what I did to Wayne."

"I thought maybe you came cause you wanted to say you were sorry," Diane says.

"I'm not sorry. He hit you, he treated you like a dog, and you..."

"You can't help who you love, Katherine. And for good or bad, I loved him. And you burnt him alive. You turned on the gas and you lit a match. You murdered him in cold blood."

"I did it for you."

"No. What you did, you did for yourself. I have to go back to work. Because you are my daughter, I'm not going to tell the two men sitting at the table who've been following me for the last month that you are here. But I swear to God, Katie, if I ever see you again, the first thing I will do is yell for help. Goodbye."

Kate struggles to live up to Jacob's definition of the good because her idea of the contented life is *equivalent* to her idea of the ultimate good. The contented life ultimately forms her *reference point* for the good, and she acts to obtain or preserve that ultimate good even at the cost of Wayne's life. Kate is not momentarily confused about the ethics of murder when she kills Wayne. Rather, her desire to obtain the ultimate good, the contented life, is stronger than her desire to live according to her idea of the good.

All humans are born with a reference point problem. As long as we equate a tangible object or idea with the ultimate good, the obtainment or preservation of the ultimate good will continue to form our reference point. The problem is that, in a conflict, this reference point overrides our innate sense of the good. As long as our idea of the ultimate good is a tangible object or idea, we can always be prevented from obtaining it.

Because **Kate's idea of the contented life includes Diane's well-being,** killing Wayne is Kate's only way to obtain that life. Kate kills Wayne because she hates and resents him, but her insufficient reference point for the good also plays a role in her decision. In the conflict between Kate's desire for the ultimate good and her desire to live out her idea of the good, the former wins.

Several years after Kate confronts her mom at the diner, she finds out Diane is dying of cancer. Diane is under guard at the hospital, but Tom, who is now a doctor, helps Kate sneak in to see her.

"Hi, mom. Can you hear me? Mom?" Diane opens her eyes.

"Mom?" says Kate, crying, "It's me, Katie."

"Katherine?"

"It's me, Katherine. I'm so sorry for everything I have put you though."

"Help. Help," Diane says softly.

"It's okay, mom. It's me."

"Help. Help."

In her last waking moments before potentially life-ending surgery, Diane refuses to let her daughter back into her life. Kate is sorry, but the road to reconciliation with her mother involves more than verbal apologies. Although Kate cannot bring Wayne back from the dead, the road to reconciliation begins with facing the consequences of her actions and turning herself over to the authorities.

By sneaking into her mom's hospital room, Kate shows that she still cannot face the consequences of what she has done. Only by realizing the toll her actions have taken on Diane and facing the consequences can Kate truly be sorry. Diane does not accept Kate's apology because Kate is not free to select her own road to reconciliation with Diane. Diane has been transgressed against; therefore, Diane determines the path to reconciliation, not Kate. To pay for her transgressions and be reconciled, Kate must accept this.

Redemption begins with being reconciled and freed from our unresolved past. However, the Hope of Redemption is ultimately about fulfilling our potential or *telos* as humans. To realize our potential we must somehow know that potential, and this explains the importance of *actualization.* Our desire to reach our potential is not just a stoic enterprise, however. It is motivated by the desire to establish our *value* as an individual.

As humans, we all have a sense that we are valuable and significant. Growing up, we look at the world and see that humans are the most advanced beings on the planet with dominion over the earth and animals. In light of this, we assign humans a higher value and justify our use of animals and plants as resources for survival.

But humans are not content to be generic clones. We also want to be valued for who we are as *particular* human beings. As humans we are all unique. We wish to be valued for our particularity. Our families play an important role in our actualization and in affirming our value as individuals. The love of our mother, father, and other family members affirms our value as a particular human different from all others.

However we cannot remain babies, loved and valued by our family, forever. We are all born with a potential yet to be realized. This potential separates us from other humans. Through realizing our potential, we establish our value as a particular male or female.

A vital element in realizing our potential is transitioning from a boy or a girl into a man or a woman. As humans we are either male or female in appearance and essence. The process of becoming a man or a woman involves physical growth and development and becoming competent in various life skills; it is also about ongoing interpretation, unlocking the inner essence of being a man or a woman.

The essence of being a man or a woman has to be unlocked because we cannot know elements of self until we reach a certain stage of maturity. Males cannot develop confidence and strength until they achieve a certain level of life skill competence. A female cannot nurture until she reaches a stage of emotional and relational maturity. Both males and females cannot know their sexual nature until puberty or adolescence.

Coming into man or womanhood does not happen in a vacuum of self-understanding, however; one ultimately has to *prove* man or womanhood to other men or women. Movies like *Braveheart* (1995) and *Fight Club* (1999) center on the male quest to prove and be affirmed in one's masculinity, while movies such as *Little Women* (1994) and *Ever After* (1998) image a woman's quest to prove and be affirmed in her femininity.

The process of becoming a man or a woman is complicated and multi-faceted. It can be very difficult to tell if someone has in fact gone through the transition. Unfortunately, not all humans enter manhood or womanhood, not even humans who become fathers or mothers themselves. How one knows that he or she has come into man or womanhood is of course difficult, but if they haven't, it is likely they will still be looking for their man or womanhood to be affirmed.

Because the process of reaching man or womanhood is somewhat uncertain, men and women need to be *authenticated* or validated by someone who has already made the journey. Only someone who has completed the rite of passage can know if someone else has done so. Man or womanhood is usually bestowed by the father or mother, and in some cultures an elaborate ritual or ceremony, particularly for males, accompanies this process.

An essential part of entering man or womanhood is gaining a basic knowledge of who one is as an individual. One does not become a generic man or woman but an individual with his or her own particularities. Developing and actualizing involves relating to other people and friends, but it is ultimately about being true to who we are as an individual. At times, we must leave groups and friends as we develop. As we approach full maturity, however, our friends will tend to remain constant.

Reaching our potential means operating at our full capacity as a human, establishing our individual value, and achieving different levels of contentment. To be fully content is to live in a perfect world and fully reach one's potential. As humans, we are always in a process of being and becoming because we each have so much potential. If freedom is a continuum, so too is human contentment.

Being human is demanding because we all want to realize our potential. We all need ongoing authentication to confirm that we are accomplishing this. Awards, prizes, positions, and trophies are important in authentication, as are words of affirmation from people who have succeeded in the relevant disciplines.

It is because our ongoing contentment always relates to realizing our potential that we face a problem as humans. Although we are free to choose our idea of the contented life, we cannot decide on our individual potential. I may decide that my idea of the contented life is being the starting goaltender for the Vancouver Canucks, but a single practice session with some fourth-line goons would reveal that my idea and my actual potential do not line up. While I am free to dream, the reality is that I do not have the potential to fulfill my fantasy.

As humans, we have a reference point problem in our selection of the ultimate good and in how we reach our full potential. There are many things we can do in life, but there are some we can do better than others. It is demanding to be human: while there are so many paths, there is no way we can walk all of them. In order to make the best choices in life, we need a complete understanding of ourselves and the world in which we live. Because no human has such understanding, it is difficult to make the best choices.

Not only is it difficult to know the best path, it is difficult to complete the path we believe fulfills our potential. Even if I had the potential to be an elite goaltender in my youth, the path to realizing that potential and getting signed by the Canucks or any NHL team is very difficult. I would have to begin at least a twenty-year journey from a very young age. Along the way, I would have to spend thousands of hours learning the trade, endure great pain and discouragement, and somehow connect with the right people to assist me.

It is because it is so difficult to make the best choices in life that each human needs to be *activated*; to have the ability to make choices beyond our own intelligence and wisdom. The ability to make these choices depends on communication with an external source who knows our potential and has complete knowledge about how we can fulfill our potential and make the best possible choices. The person or source who can guide us in reaching our full potential is known as an *activator* and this activator becomes our reference point in determining the path we should walk.

At the age of fifty, Bilbo seemed content with his lot. Apart from the annoying Sackville Baggins, who always had their eye on Bag-End, he is happy to spend nights by the fire, have the occasional ale at the *Green Dragon,* and smoke the Shire's best pipe-weed. Indeed, Bilbo is so content that the idea of going off on an adventure with a man in a grey scarf seems utterly ridiculous.

On the day he meets Gandalf, Bilbo almost doesn't realize that the man in the grey scarf is Gandalf. He treats him more like a passing hobo than a famous wizard. Bilbo is glad to see the back of him, and he hopes Gandalf will not respond to his token invitation to tea.

In contrast, when Gandalf meets the hobbit, blowing smoke rings, he knows that Bilbo is living well below his potential. Undeterred by Bilbo's treatment, Gandalf is unwilling to let Bilbo remain so far below his potential. Gandalf knows he needs to get Bilbo away from Bag-End and by scratching a sign on Bilbo's door, he gives Bilbo a solid push toward realizing his potential.

In the story of *The Lord of the Rings*, J.R.R. Tolkien is the activator. Through Gandalf, Tolkien steps into the story and guides Bilbo to realize his potential and fulfill his destiny on Middle Earth. Tolkien is the activator because he has complete knowledge of Bilbo and Middle Earth; therefore, he is able to guide and help Bilbo make the best choices.

Instead of a cowering, grumbling hobbit, Bilbo turns into something of a hero during his adventure. Through the course of his adventure, Bilbo is forced to revise his understanding of Middle Earth. Equally important, he is forced to revise his understanding of himself. As he heads back to Bag-End after his first adventure, Gandalf tells Bilbo he is not the hobbit he used to be.

It is only through Gandalf that Bilbo can realize his potential as a hobbit; only Gandalf can tell Bilbo he is in fact reaching his potential. Complete contentment does not come to Bilbo until he leaves to go to Valinor, but through his adventure, he develops a better understanding of himself and what it means to be a hobbit. An adventure with a dithering wizard was the last thing Bilbo wanted, but it turned out to be the best thing that ever happened to him.

# CHAPTER 12

## *Mercer and Beyond*

Raindrops dotted the windscreen as Nate attempted to start The Bug. If it didn't start now, it was going to be a long, wet walk to the nearest pay phone. Oncoming cars flew by as the moment of truth arrived. Nate turned the key.

To our relief, The Bug roared to life. Nate revved the engine, and began turning The Bug around; before long we were back on the highway motoring east. The fact that we had just spun out and almost crashed was hard not to talk about—an elephant in The Bug—but Nate remained silent. Throughout the trip, he responded similarly to other gaffes, such as getting chased out of the Atlanta city park and the Hooters incident. In being with Nate during these experiences it was obvious to both of us who was at fault, but Nate found it difficult to admit his error.

For Nate, gaffes like these were a setback in his quest to enter manhood. Manhood means so much more than being competent at driving but for Nate, that was one of the prerequisites. Mistakes like this one were stark reminders that he was further from manhood than he thought. Although we never saw Tony make a driving gaffe, his response to The Bug spinning out would have been different.

Tony was actually one of the best drivers I ever encountered. He was able to drive his Toyota utility using his knees with no hands on the steering wheel. Driving into the chaotic Atlanta flea market with a fully-laden truck was a walk in the park. A driving gaffe would not be seen as a threat to his manhood—Tony knew he was already there. He would have sincerely apologized, confidently moved on—and maybe even laughed about it.

Although Tony had well and truly reached manhood, many of the things that were supposed to symbolize manhood were strangely absent from his life. Instead of driving a large, manly truck, he drove a small Toyota utility. Tony drove it because it was reliable and ran well—anything on top of that was unnecessary. Tony did have a great-looking girlfriend, but he never made much of it to Nate and me, other than shifting the fan into our room at night.

In fact, apart from his girlfriend, one could be forgiven for thinking at first glance that Tony was something of a failure. Living in a hippie shack and scrapping for money at the flea market with the likes of Nate and me was likely not Tony's ideal situation. In spite of this, he was completely secure in his manhood. Tony was unlike anyone Nate and I had ever met.

In Atlanta, Nate would start all manner of conversation in an effort to understand Tony. These attempts left Nate intrigued and frustrated, but we actually got a lot out of Tony: stories from childhood, spiritual encounters, life blunders such as buying TVs filled with rocks. I was also curious about Tony, but less than Nate. Tony had won my respect as an individual and as a man, and I didn't feel I had to figure him out.

As I reflect upon my Atlanta days some fourteen years later, I realize my experience with Tony was a foundational part of my actualization and maturation into manhood. I didn't realize it at the time, but a great deal was transacted during my stay with Tony. Having an absent father left large gaps in my personal development as a man and as an individual. Even though I was unaware of it, these gaps were being filled through my relationship with Tony.

At the flea market, Tony did more than teach Nate and me how to tie ropes and sell antiques—he enabled us to grow into manhood. Even though Tony was far more competent at selling, he treated Nate and me as if we were equal partners in the venture. By showing faith in us, Tony helped us step further into maturity.

Tony had a way of looking beyond where people were and seeing who they were becoming. Although Tony was older and more experienced, I felt he always related equally to me. Tony didn't have to prove himself or appear above where I was. Rather than feeling I needed to earn my place, I felt in relating to Tony that I could be exactly myself. I began to believe that I no longer had to conform to what people expected—as an individual, I was being authenticated.

Working at a flea market was entirely different from painting. Rather than bearing the impossible burden of performing a job for which we weren't equipped, Nate and I earned just as much doing lighter work we liked better. In going along with Tony and trusting him, Nate and I found something for which we were better suited.

Through living with Tony, Nate and I discovered a new way to live. Rather than accumulating material wealth and moving up ladders, Tony's focus in life was investing in people and enabling them to be the person they were meant to be. Tony didn't have to hang out at the hostel or offer us a place to stay—he already had a girlfriend and lots of friends. Nate and I didn't have much to offer, but Tony knew there was a lot *he* could offer us at a vital stage in our development.

Nate and I didn't make a fortune at the flea market, and we lived in modest circumstances. Yet, I felt more content that summer than any other. I knew life with Tony was only temporary, but during the month in Atlanta I almost forgot I was doing a degree in mechanical engineering. I wasn't about to quit my major; I liked engineering. However, I began to see success as becoming who I was meant to be rather than achieving goals or accumulating possessions.

As the sun began to set, we motored through Indiana. Our

adventure was ending. In one day we would be back in Mercer. It was sad, but as I looked through the cracked windscreen, I felt a surge of excitement. I was confident things were going to be better.

"I don't know about you, man, but I'm getting hungry," said Nate as we passed some tempting road signs.

"Yeah, if only the Treasure Island buffet was nearby!"

"No kiddin' man; I miss Vegas already—but I saw a sign back there for Burger King, about four clicks ahead at the next exit."

"Good enough for me."

Nate turned off and parked. Before long we were eating in the familiar ambience of Burger King. We were a long way from the Las Vegas buffets, in both distance and quality, but all that seemed like a different reality as Nate and I unwrapped our food. Biting into my burger, I looked outside at the unlikely vehicle that had taken us so far.

"I think the folks back home are going to get quite the shock seeing us roll up in that thing," said Nate with a tinge of laughter. "Not many folks know The Bus died."

"Who would have believed that thing could take us around the country?" I said.

"Not many, man, trust me. I didn't believe it at the farm in Georgia."

"So why did we decide to buy it?"

"I don't know. It didn't make sense to me either, but it's turned out to be one of the best decisions we made. I think once we got past the appearance and preconceived ideas, we saw The Bug was the real deal."

The Bug *was* the real deal. Apart from some loose wires, it served us well. In spite of its imperfections, The Bug had been a godsend, neglected throughout its history but still functional and able to rescue us from some difficult situations.

"I wonder how Tony and John got along on their road trip," said Nate, moving onto the onion rings.

"Yeah, I've been thinking about that too."

"Tony was a character…I mean…can you believe that guy?" Nate rolled his eyes slightly.

"I don't know…I liked him. I'm glad we were able to stay with him."

"It's hard to believe all that really happened," Nate said.

"What's hard to believe?"

"Well, kind of everything…our whole experience in Atlanta, I just didn't expect our time to be anything like what it turned out to be. We came to Atlanta to paint a house and we ended living with Tony and selling antiques at a flea market!"

Despite his "Crazy Nate" nickname, Nate sometimes struggled with the unpredictable nature of our trip. He had more definite ideas about what he hoped to get out of the trip and liked to see himself as planner and director. At certain times, however, it seemed someone else was running the show, especially in Atlanta.

Tony was a lasting enigma for both of us. After being in our lives for a month, he'd given us a good deal to think about. Tony was a mystery and a challenge for Nate; he saw Nate for he was and who he wasn't. Nate was pushing hard to come into manhood and Tony knew that at times he had to intervene to ensure Nate didn't get ahead of himself.

While Nate was focused on entering manhood, I was more focused on finding myself. Tony was a challenge for me too, but in a different way. He was one of the most contented individuals I had ever met, yet we had hugely different ideas of success. Further, Tony had an entirely different world view. Before I met him, I had never met anyone who affirmed radical ideas such as the Bible being true or God creating the world. Yet, here was a guy I had a lot of respect for who was completely confident in these apparently insane beliefs.

I really didn't know what to do with Tony's beliefs. I thought that all sane people like me believed in evolution. The idea that God created the world and made Adam and Eve, the first humans, felt like a fantasy. But even though it was all very difficult to believe, I was okay with Tony believing it. The spiritual reading I'd done prior to the trip initiated a change in me. Previously, I might have challenged Tony. Now, I found it easier to accept people with different ideas.

"I guess we better get movin' here, man," said Nate, finishing his drink. "I think I saw a sign for a rest stop about ten miles ahead."

"Our last night on the road."

"Yeah man, hopefully it will be a good one."

We vacated Burger King and climbed back into The Bug. Just as Nate predicted we saw signs ahead for the rest stop; we parked and began setting up for the night. Nate found a nearby tree and I took my customary spot in the back. As usual, sleep came fast. There were no interruptions, and at the sound of cars pulling into the rest stop the next morning I woke and went to find Nate.

"I'm gonna miss this, man," Nate said, stretching out. "You can't beat sleeping out in the open and seeing the sun rise. How'd you sleep?"

"Good, though it's beginning to smell a bit in The Bug."

"Yeah, no kiddin'. I think the last time we did laundry was San Diego. Be good to get home and do some washing. Anyway, let's get packed and get on the road. Maybe we can make Mercer sometime this afternoon."

After we had cleaned and eaten, we were ready to embark. The day began without a hitch; The Bug started easily and ate up the miles. By the afternoon we were in Ohio seeing signs for Youngstown, the largest town before Mercer. There weren't as many signs counting down to Mercer, but soon enough we came to the exit. In around fifteen minutes we were going to be home. Nate took the turn. Before long, familiar trees and buildings approached.

"Not long now, man," Nate said.

We took the final turn and found ourselves motoring along the familiar streets of Mercer. There were a few glances at The Bug, but most people seemed oblivious to the odd-looking vehicle rolling through town. Nothing seemed to have changed except the old diner, which had been packed up and shipped off to Germany. After a few more turns we caught sight of the house.

"There it is!" said Nate. "Still lookin' good."

"Do you think anyone will be around?" I asked.

"We'll see."

Undetected, we rolled into the driveway and Nate switched off the engine.

We were back in Mercer.

Nate got out and went inside. News spread that we had returned, and before long a crowd gathered. At first glance, the appearance of The Bug suggested that our trip had been something of a train wreck—the clean white Bus replaced by a vehicle that looked at home in a junkyard. Nate told stories of our adventure to the gathering crowd, happy to be the centre of attention.

After we had greeted everyone we unloaded The Bug. Within a half-hour, sleep mats and bags, clothes, a box of laundry powder, sombreros and other random articles littered the driveway—the unconventional nature of our trip vividly illustrated by the collage of items. Some things had been lost, including The Bus and the jigsaw puzzle, but we'd returned in good health.

Nate was excited to be home, but "home" also meant reality and familiar tensions. As much as we had experienced and accomplished, Nate wanted more. His long-awaited chance to experience the freedom for which he longed was over, as was his chance to fulfill his wild desires. Such were his expectations that it would have been hard for *any* summer trip to satisfy him.

One of Nate's expectations was for us to come back with loads of money. We had by no means turned a profit on the trip (it could be argued that we suffered a hefty loss by not coming back in The Bus), but for me the wealth lay in our experiences. I had seen a lot of the United States, but I felt something more significant had happened—it felt like we had been away for years rather than months.

The next day I had breakfast with Nate and his family, who were still getting used to us being back. Nate was so animated in his storytelling that I wondered if his family actually believed anything he was saying. Whether they did or not, it was entertaining. Nate was as much an enigma for them as he remained for me.

After breakfast, we loaded up and set out for State College. I wanted to see Uncle Synick again, but Nate had a lot to do (including justifying to the exchange of The Bus for The Bug to his Dad) and I didn't want to burden him. I had a good experience in Mercer, and I was content for it to come to a close.

Nate's Dad had some doubts about The Bug being road legal in Pennsylvania, so he offered us his car. After I gathered and stowed my things, it was time to say goodbye to Nate's family. It was somewhat awkward because I had only arrived back the day prior, but I had to leave at some point. As Nate drove us away, I watched his family disappear along with the large blue house that had been my summer home.

Our route to State College was the same one we had taken in May in The Bus. A different mood prevailed as we came to terms with our adventure's end. After three hours of driving, familiar buildings approached: State College.

"Well, here we are, man," said Nate as we drove along Beaver Avenue.

"It seems like a different place without all the students."

"Yeah, it's barely August—not gonna be much action here until September. Where you stayin' again?"

"I'm staying with my friend Dave; take the next left."

Dave was a friend of Patrick, a friend of mine from Australia who had done an exchange year at Penn State a few years prior. It was Patrick who got me thinking about doing an exchange to the States; he and I were quite similar, so in some ways it felt like Dave and I were old friends.

A few minutes later Nate parked in front of Dave's apartment. It was finally time for Nate and me to go our separate ways.

"Well, it's been an adventure, man. I'm glad we did the trip together," Nate said.

"Me too—thanks for inviting me."

"No worries; I think it worked out well."

"Enjoy the rest of the summer in Mercer."

"I'll try; I've got a lot to take care of before school starts up. What are you going to get up to in State College?"

"I don't know. I'll see what happens."

"You could always do a trip or something—you're not that far from Philadelphia and the airport."

"Yeah, we'll see. If I get restless, that's always an option."

"Anyway, man, I need to hit the road here and get my dad's car back, but I'll see you in September."

After a solid handshake and a final farewell, Nate drove away down the street. For the first time in three months we were apart. I moved my things into the spare room at Dave's, which also contained the boxes I had left at the beginning of the summer—they felt like remnants of a distant life. Hard to believe I was soon going to be immersed in textbooks and equations again— but a part of me looked forward to the familiar lifestyle.

Dave worked on campus, so we mostly hung out at night leaving my days relatively free. It was good to be back at State College without the rigors of being a full-time student. I bought some more spirituality books, registered for courses, and visited some familiar haunts. But after several days I grew restless.

Two months on the road should have been enough to quench my traveling desires. At the time, it was hard to understand what was driving me—the summer adventure awoke something in me, and I found it hard to stay put. I felt like I was close to finding something, and that I was somehow being driven toward it. With almost a month of free time on my hands, I could do nothing but go on another adventure.

During our trip, Nate gave me glowing reviews of Jamaica and Jamaican bud. I hadn't intended to go, but the idea grew on me after seeing advertisements for cheap flights. As an Australian, Jamaica always seemed so far away. Now it was close and relatively inexpensive.

Prior to my summer adventure, I doubt that I would have entertained the option of flying to Jamaica by myself for a week. But during my trip with Nate I developed more confidence at traveling. Nate and I had traveled for two months with minimal planning and somehow it all worked out—even the death of The Bus didn't stop our adventure. I was so confident that I also planned to cycle to Philadelphia from State College, inspired by a guy we met who had ridden his bike from Miami to Wyoming.

Nate and I met the cyclist at a rest stop driving home. I can't remember his reason for making the trip, but I remember being blown away by how far the cyclist had come. He looked fit and well, probably in the best shape of his life, and it was inspiring to meet him. Usually, we were the ones doing the inspiring, but this encounter reversed the roles. The cyclist made such an impression that Nate made a cross-country bicycle trip the next summer.

After a day mulling over Jamaica, I decided to go ahead. I

bought a plane ticket to Montego Bay, flying out of Philadelphia to save money. The thought of being on the road again excited me. I could have taken a bus, but biking seemed much more interesting. My plan was to bike to Philadelphia and then take the bus back. It was ambitious but it was less than two-hundred miles to Philadelphia, nothing compared to riding a bike from Miami to Wyoming.

My plan was to ride along the main highway. Dave suggested I take back roads, but looking at the map I saw that meant a considerable diversion. In those pre-cell phone days, I was reluctant to get too far off the beaten track. I didn't know the road regulations concerning cyclists on highways, but a two-hundred mile bike trip seemed fine to me.

At a relaxed pace, I calculated that at 30-40 miles a day it would take a week at most to complete the ride. All I needed was an inexpensive bike, a tent and a few other items for the road. I accumulated the basic necessities and did some practice rides around State College. My excitement mounted as I imagined the upcoming adventure.

All was in order when the big day arrived. Another clear summer's day beckoned as I loaded up my bike, said goodbye to Dave, and began pedaling. Familiar landscape slowly disappeared behind me. After coasting down a series of long hills, I knew I had passed the point of no return.

The first day was a success. The miles to Philadelphia ticked down, and I was ahead of schedule by lunchtime, building up a cushion of about 10 miles by dinner. I found a place to camp near a highway exit; after pitching my tent, I laid down and contemplated my first day on the road. Numerous roadside camp outs with Nate had made me an expert.

I awoke early the next morning, took down the tent, and loaded up my bike. I was doing so well that by lunchtime I had reached my target and decided to stop at a small town where I could buy some food and find a place to camp. I'd been worried about my first long bike trip, but at this rate I would reach Philadelphia in no time.

The next morning I went about my usual routine, but after a few hours on the bike traffic got busier. I neared Harrisburg—halfway there. My plan was to get through the city and ride until mid-afternoon. I'd have liked a quieter route, but without a detailed map the highway felt easier. As the number of exits increased, I had to be careful to check for cars turning.

All was going well that morning until I felt a solid thud—then darkness. The next thing I remember was waking up on the side of the road with my bike and belongings scattered over the pavement. Cars and trucks stopped on either the side of the road, piling up chaotically around the accident. As I came to my senses, I had no idea how I'd ended up prone on the side of the road. One minute I was steadily progressing to Philadelphia, the next I was staring up at clouds.

As I sat up and took everything in, the accident and surrounding chaos somehow became secondary. I had an awareness of things I had never know before—like waking after a long sleep. I was conscious of everything going on around me, but something more important seemed to be happening. People jumped out of their cars to check on me; the moment passed. But there was no denying its strangeness.

I sat up, relieved that I hadn't suffered any major injuries. As I looked around, I saw a maroon truck parked close behind me. I was always careful about checking the exits, but I didn't count on this truck making a very late turn and cutting through the white paint. I was well past the entry point when I was hit. As I stood up to survey the wreckage, I thought for a moment that I might be able to get on my bike and continue. Then I saw the large scrapes on my hips and legs and my bike's buckled wheel. The biking was over.

A small argument was developing between the driver who had hit me and the other drivers. It was obvious from where he had stopped that he was at fault, but even though the driver was negligent, I wasn't sure if I was supposed to be riding on the side of the highway. Given that I had no serious injuries and didn't like being the centre of attention, I just wanted to leave. I had medical insurance, and with my inexpensive bike only a little worse for wear I didn't feel like making a claim against the driver.

After telling him I was okay he took off, leaving myself and the others who had stopped. The bystanders weren't happy; one, a registered nurse, offered to drive me to the hospital to get me checked out. Initially reluctant, scrapes the size of my hand convinced me. Accompanied by his wife, the nurse drove me to the hospital.

There, I was taken to the emergency room and put through some tests. Apart from the scrapes, I was in good health. After getting disinfected and bandaged, I was told I didn't need to stay in the hospital: I could rest up at a hotel. The couple was waiting for me when I emerged and offered to drive me.

In the space of one hour I had gone from pedaling to Philadelphia to sitting in a hotel room in Harrisburg with my beaten-up bike. It was a remarkable transition. The couple returned several times to the hotel with medical supplies; I offered to pay them but they refused. In all my life, I have yet to receive this kind of hospitality from strangers.

Once at the hotel, my job was to rest, periodically change my bandaging, and disinfect my grazes. Pouring disinfectant on large scrapes was enough to bring me to my knees, but I was thankful that I wasn't seriously injured. In between changing bandages, I watched movies on HBO and thought about the strange awareness I experienced after waking up from the accident.

As I reflected, I felt I had to make a decision. There was something important and obvious I had glossed over. It was time to stop escaping and begin thinking, to stop and consider what lay behind the summer's bizarre nature. I had been willing to interpret everything as mere coincidence. Now, that seemed inadequate.

My thoughts naturally returned to Atlanta and Tony. I had no idea where he was or how I could contact him. The only link I had was the book to which he had such strong ties: the Bible. Whatever my preconceptions, this book was my only link to Tony and my only clue to what had happened after the crash. In the past, I had built up so much resistance to this book; I was on track to read every spiritual book *except* the Bible.

Now I had to read it. After a night at the hotel, I felt better and was able to move without much pain. I resolved to go downtown in search of the mysterious book. There was likely a Bible in the room's dresser, but at the time I had no idea that might be the case. In Harrisburg, I found a small bookstore with a whole shelf devoted to Bibles. I picked out an interesting-looking Men's Devotional Bible and returned to the hotel. Excited, I lay on my bed and started reading.

*In the beginning God created the heavens and the earth…* Most of the self-help books I read began with "you." This one began with God. As I read, I was offered no promises or benefits. I was merely a spectator to God's creation: the sun, the earth, creatures, plants.

*Then God said, "Let us make man in our image, after our likeness…"* The reference to "us" confused me. Nevertheless God declared everything he had made good, including humans. He proceeded to rest on the seventh day. In the space of a few pages, this God had made everything that exists. But instead of humans living happily ever after, they ate from the forbidden tree. Things seemed to go sideways.

It was an unusual book. I read through a long genealogy, a devastating flood, the building of a large tower, and the scattering of humans over the face of the earth. *Now the Lord said to Abram, "Go from your country and your kindred and your father's house and to the land that I will show you…"* The story took a sudden turn at the end of Chapter Eleven, narrowing in on a character named Abram who always seemed to be traveling. I didn't know how this quest to enter a promised land related to me, but as I read I experienced an excitement unlike any I had ever known.

*I will multiply your offspring as the stars of heaven and will give to your offspring all these lands. And in your offspring all the nations of the earth shall be blessed…* before long I had read halfway through Genesis. It was lunchtime. I didn't know if what I was reading had actually happened, but this book offered an important clue as to the thing I was trying to find. After years without any clear idea of what I was seeking, I now had a definite sense that I was close to finding it. I was excited.

After several days at the hotel and numerous movies, I had read though the book of Genesis and was ready to leave. My flight to Jamaica was five days away, and I was keen to see Philadelphia. After getting my bike and possessions into boxes, I cabbed and bussed it to Philadelphia.

The bright sunny weather in Philadelphia reflected my mood. After years spent wandering, I felt close to finding what I was looking for. Events that summer held a continuity; they seemed to lead me somewhere. I didn't know where the Bible was taking me, but it was a new and exciting clue.

The hostel in Philadelphia was cozy, well-run, and opposite a Presbyterian Church. I knew there was a connection between the Bible and churches so I was eager to attend. After a lifetime of ignoring churches, I now had an interest. I had been to a Catholic church earlier that year with my friend Ryan but never on my own accord. The next day happened to be Sunday, and I planned to attend.

I woke up excited about the morning service. It was a clear, sunny day and considerably quieter around the hostel. The church was about half full when I entered. I sat in the wooden pews a safe distance from the front. A likeable middle-aged woman presided over the service; the sermon concerned Jesus walking on water.

*But when the disciples saw him walking on the sea, they*

*were terrified, and said, "It is a ghost!" and they cried out in fear. But immediately Jesus spoke to them, saying, "Take heart; it is I. Do not be afraid."* As I listened, I found it hard to believe the events had actually happened. Walking on water went against everything I had learned in physics and fluid mechanics class.

*"Lord, if it is you, command me to come to you on the water." He said, "Come." So Peter got out of the boat and walked on the water and came to Jesus...* In many ways I felt like I was being asked to walk on water, doing things I had never imagined. Reading the Bible was as irrational as it got. Walking into a church was even crazier. I didn't know if the story was true, but I was impacted by Peter's struggle with faith.

I found the pastor after the service and thanked her for the sermon. I was encouraged by what I had heard, more significantly, I felt at peace while attending the church. In my personal struggles, peace had been a rare commodity. I loved being able to solve problems, but these dilemmas had proven unsolvable. There seemed to be no escape from my inner tensions.

After church I went to the Philadelphia Museum of Art. I didn't know much about the museum: it was important and it had a statue of Rocky Balboa out front. This was the first time I had gone to a major museum and I was amazed. I had never seen old paintings and artifacts before, and I was especially taken by the religious paintings.

As I toured the museum, characters from the Bible stared out at me from the walls. I began to wonder if these people had really existed. The artists who painted these pictures, the geniuses of their time, chose to paint characters and events from the Bible.

There was no escaping that in a previous age the artists, or whoever paid them, believed the characters and events described in the Bible were central to their understanding of reality.

At the museum, I felt like I was in a different world. The events and characters in the mysterious book I was reading became real, and I found myself wanting to spend time with them. This new world excited me so much that I went back three more times before leaving for Jamaica. I was walking on water and I liked it. I wasn't sure how Jesus and his disciples fit into Abraham's story, but I was excited about my daily meeting with all these new characters each day at the museum.

I enjoyed Philadelphia so much that I had half a mind to stay, but there was no turning back. After four days I was looking forward to experiencing the Caribbean for the first time. With my bike and belongings stored at the hostel, I checked out and took a cab to the airport. On the plane, I took out my Bible and started reading. This mysterious book became more compelling every day, but I was still lost at sea in terms of my understanding.

After take off, the man sitting next to me asked me about what I was reading. He discerned quickly that I had no idea and told me he was a missionary to Jewish people. I wasn't sure why Jewish people needed missionaries, but he seemed to know a great deal about the Bible. Before I knew it I was being led through a prayer which was supposed to make me a follower of this book—a Christian.

After the prayer, the man wrote out a long list of verses for me to read, mostly from the Book of John, which I learned was from the second part of the Bible: the New Testament. When the plane landed in Montego Bay, I suddenly found myself a believer of the book—a Christian. The man wished me well; I thanked him for helping me. I wasn't any closer to understanding what being a follower of the book meant, but I was excited that I was now a member of the club.

My hotel was cheap and non-descript, but adequate. There were quite a few Westerners staying there, and because it was a small hotel I got to know some of them during my stay, including Troy, a policeman from New Zealand there on vacation, and a young couple from Chicago; the guy had been recently reading the Bible as well. Most of the hotel guests were in a similar phase of life, and we spent a lot of time talking, drinking, and smoking.

One day, I took a trip to an exotic beach up the coast. Apart from the crowded bus, it was a good day: the beach was exactly as advertised. My time in Jamaica was not without drama, however. I was near a bank robbery and street shootout in Montego Bay, and I was almost robbed at knife-point while walking in town with Troy. Both of us were backed up against a wall when Troy grabbed the mugger's hand; he had it behind his back in an instant. The speed and ease with which Troy did this was something to behold—almost like he was shelling peas. The mugger ran away. Not wanting any further drama we hastened back to the hotel and stayed local for the duration of the trip.

After six days in Montego Bay, I was due to fly back to Philadelphia. The couple from Chicago had departed a few days prior and Troy had left that morning; it seemed like a fitting time to go. Seeing my Jamaica friends leave saddened me. We had built solidarity through all the drama, and we'd had a great time hanging out at the hotel. That night when no one was around, I read avidly through the list of scriptures I had been given on the plane. They spoke of new life, of being saved from one's sins, and this person— Jesus. It made no sense to me, but now that I was a believer I wanted to solve the riddle.

The plane ride back to Philadelphia was quiet and uneventful. I was thankful to be heading to relative safety. I spent the night at the hostel, happy to be back in the city which had helped me become a believer. The next morning, I caught the bus back to State College.

On the bus, I felt like Bilbo returning to Bag-End after his first adventure. There was no Gandalf to confirm that I was different, but I knew the summer had changed me. As familiar scenery passed by, I felt like I was entering a promised land of sorts. There was still much to sort out in terms of what I believed, but after years of being lost I knew I was on the right path.

Back at State College, I began attending weekly meetings of Christian Student Fellowship. Through the course of the semester and one-on-one meetings with the group leader, Buzz Roberts, I began to understand what being a Christian was about. On November 11th, 1996, I was baptized. Like the Losties, it was a community in need of redemption, but through being a part of it I was able to begin my own path to redemption.

# Select Bibliography

As the heading suggests the following is not a comprehensive bibliography of this complex and multidimensional nature of this work. Although this is not a comprehensive list, the following works are listed in the spirit of responsible declaration of the works consulted in the writing of this book.

Adams, Douglas. *The Ultimate Hitchhiker's Guide:The Hitchhiker's Guide to the Galaxy.* New York: Random House, 1996.
_____. *The Ultimate Hitchhiker's Guide: The Restaurant at the End of the Universe.* New York: Random House, 1996.
Aquinas, Thomas. *Summa Theologica.* Vol. 1,2,3. Translated by Fathers of the English Dominican Province. Notre Dame: Christian Classics, 1981.
Anselm of Canterbury. *The Major Works.* Edited by Brian Davies. *Why God Became Man* Translated by Camilla McNab. New York: Oxford University Press, 1998.
Aristotle. *The Basic Works of Aristotle.* Edited by Richard McKeon. *Metaphysics.* Translated by W. D. Ross. New York : Random House, 1941.
_____. *The Basic Works of Aristotle.* Edited by Richard McKeon. *On The Heavens.* Translated by J. L. Stocks. New York : Random House, 1941.
_____. *The Basic Works of Aristotle.* Edited by Richard McKeon. *Nicomachean Ethics.* Translated by W. D. Ross. New York : Random House, 1941.
_____. *The Basic Works of Aristotle.* Edited by Richard McKeon. *Politics.* Translated by Benjamin Jowett. New York : Random House, 1941.
_____. *The Basic Works of Aristotle.* Edited by Richard McKeon. *Physics.* Translated by R.P. Hardie and R. K. Gaye. New York: Random House, 1941.
_____. *The Basic Works of Aristotle.* Edited by Richard McKeon. *On Generation and Corruption.* Translated by Harold H. Joachim. New York: Random House, 1941.
_____. *The Basic Works of Aristotle.* Edited by Richard McKeon. *On the Soul.* Translated by J.A. Smith. New York: Random House, 1941.
_____. *The Basic Works of Aristotle.* Edited by Richard McKeon. *On the Generation of Animals.* Translated by Arthur Platt. New York: Random House, 1941.
Augustine. *Nicene and Post-Nicene Fathers,* 1st Series. Vol 3. Edited by Philip Schaff.

*On The Holy Trinity.* Translated by Arthur Haddan. Peabody: Hendrickson Publishers, 2004.
_____. *Nicene and Post-Nicene Fathers,* 1st Series. Vol 2. Edited by Philip Schaff.
*The City of God.* Translated by Marcus Dods. Peabody: Hendrickson Publishers, 2004.
_____. *Nicene and Post-Nicene Fathers,* 1st Series. Vol 1. Edited by Philip Schaff.
*The Confessions.* Translated by J.G. Pilkington. Peabody: Hendrickson Publishers, 2004.

Barth, Karl. *Church Dogmatics: Doctrine of the Word of God 1.1.* Edited by Bromiley and Torrance. Translated by G.W. Bromiley. London: T & T Clark International, 2004
_____. *Church Dogmatics: Doctrine of the Word of God 1.2.* Edited by Bromiley and Torrance. Translated by G.W. Bromiley. London: T & T Clark International, 2004
_____. *Church Dogmatics: Doctrine of God 2.1.* Edited by Bromiley and Torrance. Translated by G.W. Bromiley. London: T & T Clark International, 2004
_____. *Church Dogmatics: Doctrine of God 2.2.* Edited by Bromiley and Torrance. Translated by G.W. Bromiley. London: T & T Clark International, 2004
_____. *The Epistle to the Romans.* Translated by Edwyn C. Hoskins. London: Oxford University Press, 1968.

Copleston, Frederick. *History of Philosophy:Greece and Rome.* Vol 1. New York: Image Books, 1993.
_____. *History of Philosophy:Medieval Philosophy.* Vol 2. New York: Image Books, 1993.
_____. *History of Philosophy:Late Medieval and Renaissance Philosophy.* Vol 3. London: Continuum, 2003.
_____. *History of Philosophy:Modern Philosophy: From Descartes to Leibniz.* Vol 4. New York: Image Books, 1993.
_____. *History of Philosoph:British Philosophy:Hobbes to Hume.* Vol 5. London: Continuum, 2003.
_____. *History of Philosophy:Modern Philosophy: From the French Enlightenment to Kant.* Vol 6. New York: Image Books, 1993.
_____. *History of Philosophy:Modern Philosophy: From The Post-Kantian Idealists to Marx, Kierkegaard, and Nietzsche.* Vol 7. New York: Image Books, 1993.
_____. *History of Philosophy:Modern Philosophy: Empiricism, Idealism, and Pragmatism in Britain and America.* Vol 8. New York: Image Books, 1993.
_____. *History of Philosophy:Modern Philosophy: From the French Revolution to Sartre, Camus, and Levi-Strauss.* Vol 9. New York: Image Books, 1993.

Bonaventure. *The Soul's Journey into God-The Tree of Life-The Life of St. Francis.* Edited by Richard Paybe. Translated by Ewert Cousins. New Jersey: Paulist Press, 1978.

Cohen, Alan. *Dare to be Yourself.* New York: Random House, 1991.

Dante, Alighieri. *The Divine Comedy:Volume 3:Paradise.* Translated by Mark Musa. New York: Penguin Books, 1986.

Descartes, Rene. *A Discourse on the Method.* Translation by Ian Maclean. Oxford: Oxford University Press, 2008.
_____. *Meditations on First Philosophy.* Translation by Michael Moriarty. Oxford: Oxford University Press, 2008.

Evans, Stephen. *Kierkegaard on Faith and The Self: Collected Essays.* Waco: Baylor University Press, 2006.
Freeman, Charles. *Egypt, Greece and Rome: Civilizations of the Ancient Mediterranean.* 2d ed. Oxford: Oxford University Press, 2004.
Gilson, Etienne. *The Spirit of Medieval Philosophy.* Translated by A.H.C. Downes. Oxford: Oxford University Press, 1991.
Gonzalez, Justo L. *The Story of Christianity:The Early Church to the Dawn of the Reformation.* Vol I. New York: HarperSanFrancisco, 1984.
_____. *The Story of Christianity: The Reformation to the Present Day.* Vol 2. New York: HarperSanFrancisco, 1984.
Grant, Edward. *A History of Natural Philosophy: From the Ancient World to the Nineteenth Century.* Cambridge:Cambridge University Press, 2008.
_____. *The Foundations of Modern Science in The Middle Ages:Their Religious, Institutional, and Intellectual Contexts.* Cambridge:Cambridge University Press, 2007.
Gregory of Nazianzus. *On God and Christ.* Translated by Frederick Williams and Lionel Wickam. Crestwood: St Vladimir's Press, 2002.
Gregory of Nyssa. *Nicene and Post-Nicene Fathers.* 2d Series, Vol 5. Edited by Philip Schaff. *On The Making of Man.* Translated by H.A Wilson. Peabody: Hendrickson Publishers, 2004.
_____. *Nicene and Post-Nicene Fathers.* 2d Series, Vol 5. Edited by Philip Schaff. *On The Soul and Resurrection.* Translated by H.A Wilson. Peabody: Hendrickson Publishers, 2004.
Hart, David B. *The Story of Christianity:An Illustrated History of 2000 Years of the Christian Faith.* London: Quercus, 2007.
Heidegger, Martin. *Being and Time.* Translated by J. Macquarrie and E. Robinson. New York: Harper & Row Publishers, 2008.
_____. *Introduction to Metaphysics.* Translated by G. Fried and R Polt. Yale: Yale University Press, 2000.
Hegel, Georg Wilhelm Friedrich. *Phenomenology of Spirit.* Translated by A.V. Miller. Oxford: Oxford University Press, 1977.
Hobbes, Thomas. *Leviathan.* Edited by J. Gaskin. New York: Oxford University Press, 2008.
Homer. *The Odyssey.* Translated by W. Shewring. New York: Oxford University Press, 2008.
Husserl, Edmund. *Cartesian Meditations.* Translated by Dorion Cairns. Dordrecht: Kluwer Academic Publishers, 1999.
John of Damascus. *Nicene and Post-Nicene Series,* 1st Series. Vol 9. Edited by Philip Schaff. *An Exact Exposition of the Orthodox Faith.* Translated by S.D.F. Salmond. Peabody: Hendrickson Publishers, 2004.
Kant, Immanuel. *Critique of Pure Reason.* Translated by J.M.D. Mieklejohn. Minelola: Dover Publication, 2003.
_____. *Groundwork for the Metaphysics of Morals.* Translated by T. Abbot. New York:Broadview Editions, 2005.
Kierkegaard, Soren. *Fear and Trembling.* Translation by Alastair Hannay. London: Penguin Books, 2003.
_____. *Kierkegaard's Writings,* Vol 20. Edited by H.Hong and E Hong. *Practice in*

*Christianity*. Translated by H. Hong and E Hong. Princeton: Princeton University Press, 1991.

———. *Either/Or*. Vol 1. Translated by D. Swenson. Garden City: Anchor Books edition, 1959.

Latourette, Kenneth Scott. *A History of Christianity: Beginnings to 1500*. Vol 1. Peabody: Prince Press, 1999.

———. *A History of Christianity: Reformation to the Present*. Vol 2. Peabody: Prince Press, 1999.

Lyotard, Jean-Francois. *The Postmodern Condition: A Report on Knowledge*. Translation by G. Bennington and B. Massumi. Minneapolis: University of Minnesota Press, 1984.

Macintyre, Alasdair. *A Short History of Ethics*, 2d ed. London: Routledge Classics, 1998.

———. *After Virtue*, 3d ed. Notre Dame: University of Notre Dame Press, 2007.

Machiavelli, Niccolo. *The Prince and Other Writings*. Translated by W. Rebhorn. New York: Barnes & Noble Books, 2003.

McInerney, Ralph. *Aquinas*. Cambridge: Polity Press, 2004.

Moorman, J.R.H. *A History of the Church of England*, 3d ed. Harrisburg: Morehouse Publishing, 1980.

Nietszche, Frederick. *Basic Writings of Nietzsche*. Edited and Translated by Walter Kaufman. *Beyond Good and Evil*. New York: The Modern Library, 2000.

Pelikan, Jarislav. *Acts: Brazos Theological Commentary on the Bible*. Grand Rapids: Brazos Press, 2005.

Plato. *Plato: Complete Works*. Edited by John M. Cooper. *The Republic*. Translated by G.M.A. Grube and C.D.C. Reeve. Indianapolis: Hacket Publishing Company, 1997.

———. *Plato: Complete Works*. Edited by John M. Cooper. *Timaeus*. Translated by D. Zeyl. Indianapolis: Hacket Publishing Company, 1997.

———. *Plato: Complete Works*. Edited by John M. Cooper. *Theatetus*. Translated by M. Levett and M. Burnyeat. Indianapolis: Hacket Publishing Company, 1997.

———. *Plato: Complete Works*. Edited by John M. Cooper. *Meno*. Translated by G.M.A. Grube. Indianapolis: Hacket Publishing Company, 1997.

———. *Plato: Complete Works*. Edited by John M. Cooper. *Symposium*. Translated by A. Nehamas and P. Woodruff. Indianapolis: Hacket Publishing Company, 1997.

———. *Plato: Complete Works*. Edited by John M. Cooper. *Phaedo*. Translated by G.M.A. Grube. Indianapolis: Hacket Publishing Company, 1997.

———. *Plato Complete Works*. Edited by John M. Cooper. *Crito*. Translated by G.M.A. Grube. Indianapolis: Hacket Publishing Company, 1997.

———. *Plato: Complete Works*. Edited by John M. Cooper. *Apology*. Translated by G.M.A. Grube. Indianapolis: Hacket Publishing Company, 1997.

———. *Plato: Complete Works*. Edited by John M. Cooper. *Euthyphro*. Translated by G.M.A. Grube. Indianapolis: Hacket Publishing Company, 1997.

———. *Plato: Complete Works*. Edited by John M. Cooper. *On Justice*. Translated by A. Becker. Indianapolis: Hacket Publishing Company, 1997.

Pseudo-Dionysius. *Pseudo-Dionysius: The Complete Works*. Translated by C. Luibheid. *On the Divine Names*. Mahwah: Paulist Press, 1987.

Rawls, John. *The Law of Peoples*. Cambridge: Harvard University Press, 2002.

Rieff, Philip. *The Triumph of the Therapeutic: Uses of Faith After Freud*, 40th aniv. ed.

Delaware: ISI Books, 2006.
Russel, Bertrand. *The History of Western Philosophy.* New York: Simon & Schuster, 1972.
Sartre, Jean-Paul. *Being and Nothingness.* Translated by H. Barnes. New York: Washington Square Press, 1984.
_____. *Existentialism is a Humanism.* Translated by C. Macomber. New Haven: Yale University Press, 2007.
Schopenhauer, Arthur. *The World as Will and Representation.* Vol 1. Translated by E.F.J. Payne. New York: Dover Publications, 1969.
Singer, Peter. *One World: The Ethics of Globalization,* 2d ed. London: Yale University Press, 2002.
Tolkien. J.R.R. *The Lord of the Rings.* London:Harper Collins Publishers, 1995.

_____. *The Hobbit or There and Back Again.* Boston: Houghton Mifflin Company, 2001.
_____. *The Silmarillion,* 2d ed. Boston: Houghton Mifflin Company, 2001.

# Topical Index

Abraham, 58, 248
Activation, 268
Activator, 268, 269
Actualization, 164, 208, 209, 246
  context, 246
  imperfection, 246
  process going awry, 209
Adams, Douglas, 28
  *Hitchhikers Guide to the Galaxy*, 28-29
Age of Enlightenment, 70, 116, 118, 149, 156, 213, 249
Age of Reason, 71, 214, 249
Alexander the Great, 57
Anaxagoras, 47
Animals, 211
  gap btw. humans and animals, 212
Anthropology, 43, 171
A Priori Knowledge, 172
Appian, 106
Aquinas, Thomas, 56, 65-67
  doctrine of analogy, 66, 67
Aristotle, 52, 100
  doctrine of four elements, 70
  heavenly bodies, 5
  mathematics, 70
  *Metaphysics*, 52, 100
  *Nicomachean Ethics*, 153, 250
  *Physics*, 115
  *Politics*, 148-149
  telos, 249
  translation of, 63
  unity problem, 56
  view of humans, 61
  view of matter, 61
Atheism, 112
Augustine, 59-60
  *The City of God*, 59
  universals, 60
Authentication, 266

Babylonians, 249
Barth, Karl, 102
Becket, Sister Wendy, 33
Bentham, Jeremy, 151
Bonaventure, 67
Boyle, Robert, 116
Byzantium, 60, 62

Caesar, Julius, 105
Categorical Imperative, 154, 157-158
Causality, 117, 122, 172
Cicero, 106
Charlemagne, 60
Christianity, 57, 247
Church, 58, 59, 247
Columbus, Christopher, 70
Consciousness, 218, 164
  conscience, 260
  reflective, 205, 211
Constantinople, 60
  fall of, 62
Constantine, 57, 113
Constantius II, 57
Contentment, 206, 261, 267

303

Contingency, 200, 204
  anxiety, 203
  most powerful being, 220
  sartre, 220
Corruption, 251, 257
Crusades, 62-63

Dante, Alighieri, 67
Dasein, 112
Demiurge, 49, 54, 59
Deontological Ethics, 150
Descartes, Rene, 71, 112, 115, 119, 214
Divine Law, 149

Economic Security, 204
Edict of Milan, 57
Efficient Cause, 53
Engels, Friedrich, 151
Epistemological Gap, 102, 110
Epistemology
  defn, 94
  false judgement, 96
  faith, belief, 111
  knowledge of people, 110
  knowledge of the gods, 111
  realm of knowledge, 109
  reasonable account, 107-108
  revelation, 111
Equivocal Understanding, 69
Essence, 53, 54, 117, 163
Ethics, defn, 148
Evil, 250
Existentialism, 215, 216
  effects of, 216

Faith, 111, 220
Fate, 203
Final Cause, 53
Forms, 47, 121
Formal cause, 50
Foundation of Being, 112, 218
Forgiveness, 254, 255
  supernatural, 255
Francis of Assisi, 67
Freedom, 155, 157, 171, 207
  accountability, 155, 163

Galileo, 70
General Revelation, 68, 113
Golden Mean, 156, 205
Good, 147, 148, 152, 204
  for aristotle, 204
  ultimate good, 205, 261
  idea of, 260
Greeks, 46-47
Gregory of Nazianzus, 61, 66
Gregory of Nyssa, 61

Hebrews, 247, 248
Hegel, Georg Wilhelm, 151
Heidegger, Martin, 19, 32, 215, 218
  consciousness, 218
  dasein, 218-219
Herodotus, 222
  *The Histories*, 222
Higgs Particle, 54
Hippocrates, 249
History, 222-223
Hobbes, Thomas, 150
Holy Scriptures, 61
  genesis, the book of, 58
Homer, 250
Hope, 222
Human, 159
  conception, 209
  context, 246
  dehumanizing, 170
  essence, 163, 207-208, 211
  female, 207
  identity, 164
  intimacy, 167, 168
  male, 207
  maturing, 265-267
  nakedness, 162
  nature of, 164
  non-causal motion, 163
  past, 246
  potential, 207-208, 264
  relationships, 165, 166, 206
  sexual behaviour, 160
  unveiling, 165, 166
  value, 265
  veiling, 165

Hume, David, 122
  denial of causality, 171
Husserl, Edmund, 215
Imperfection, 247
  disasters, 249
Islam, 62

Jesus of Nazareth, 58, 247
John of Damascus, 61, 66
  *Exact Exposition of The Orth. Faith,* 61

Kant, Immanuel, 112, 122, 150
  a priori, 172
  copernican revolution, 172
  divine consciousness, 172
  human freedom, 173
  individual consciousness, 172
  two-fold metaphysic, 173-174
Kepler, Johannes, 69
Kierkegaard, Soren, 102, 151, 215
  *Fear and Trembling,* 151
Knowledge
  defn, 109
  realm of, 109-110

Leibniz, Gottfried, 115
Leonardo da Vinci, 32
Locke, John, 60, 121, 171
  *A Treatise of Civil Government,* 152
  ethics, 152
  primary qualities, 121-122
  secondary qualities, 121-122
Love, 159, 255
Luther, Martin, 71

Machiavelli, Niccolo, 150
  *The Prince,* 150
Macintyre, Alasdair, 150
Magical Ont. Watch, 55, 69, 113, 212
Material cause, 50
Mathematics, 112
Martel, Charles, 62
Marx, Karl, 151
Mechanical Ont. Watch, 55, 114, 249
Medieval Age, 213

Medieval University, 63
Mesopotamia, 248
Metanarrative, 196, 250
Metaphysics, 49, 70, 117, 118, 122, 163
Mill, J.S, 150
Miracles, 117, 213
Modern Philosophy, 119, 120, 122
Mona Lisa, 32-33
Moses, 248
Muhammad, 62
Mysteries, 158-159

Natural Philosophy, 69, 113, 114, 116, 213
Newton, Isaac, 69, 115, 122
Nietzsche, Frederick, 151
  *Beyond Good and Evil,* 151, 250

Objective Knowledge, 102, 104
Ockham, William of, 69, 115
One-to-one correspondence, 115
Ontology, 113, 121
  defn, 44
  supplants metaphysics, 120
Ontological Ethics, 149

Paganism, 58
  view of humans, 58-49
Pandora's Box, 250
Parmenides, 47, 201, 218
Passions, 155
Persian Empire, 62
Phenomenology, 120, 202, 214-217
Plato, 48, 49-51, 98, 151
  gap or discontinuity, 51
  *Republic,* plato's cave, 98
  *Theatetus,* 95
  view of the humans, 51
Plutarch, 106
Pornography, 171
Postmodernism, 43
Potential, 207, 267
Prime Matter, *See* Metaphysics
Protagoras, 47
Protestant Reformation, 71

Pseudo-Dionysius, 61, 66
    divine processions, 61-62
    *On the Divine Names,* 61
Purpose, 202
    *See also* teleology

Rawls, John, 150
Realist Ethics, 150
Reason, 72, 118, 157
Reconciliation, 264
Redemption, 210, 248, 257
    defn, 247
Reference Point, 98, 117, 149
    actualization, 246
    defn, 247
    idea of the good, 263
    path to potential, 267
    words as, 215
Renaissance, 214
Revelation, 111
Romans, 57-59, 60-61

Sallust, 106
Sartre, Jean-Paul, 112, 215, 218
    causality, 220
    in-itself, 219
    for-itself, 219
    thirst, 220
Schopenhauer, Arthur, 215, 217
Scientific Revolution, 114, 115
Scotus, Duns, 69
Second Book, 61

Sex, 160-161, 169
    bodily intimacy, 169
    discrepancy, 169, 170
    relational intimacy, 169
Singer, Peter, 151
Socrates, 47
Solipsism, 216
Special Revelation, 68, 111
Subjective Knowledge, 102, 104
Substance, 50, 100

Teleology, 204
    defn, 200
Temporality, 218
Thales of Miletus, 33-34, 47
Theology, 69, 213
    doctrine of the trinity, 58
    eucharist, 159
    fall, the, 58, 250
    queen of the sciences, 69
Toledo, capture of, 63
Tours, battle of, 62

Universals, *See* forms
Univocal, 69
Unmoved Mover, 53, 59, 112
Utilitarianism, 150

Virtues, 155, 205
    character, 156
    intellectual, 156

Yahweh, 248

www.ingramcontent.com/pod-product-compliance
Lightning Source LLC
Chambersburg PA
CBHW022001160426
43197CB00007B/222